Unlock The Millionaire
Lying Dormant Inside

A Mindset Journey from
Ordinary to Extraordinary

By

Keith Henderson

I

Table of Contents

Introduction

Greetings, and a warm welcome to "Unlock The Millionaire Lying Dormant Inside: A Mindset Journey from Ordinary to Extraordinary." I'm Keith Henderson, and I'm delighted to embark on this journey with you, sharing the extraordinary path that has propelled me from a routine 12-hour nightly job to a transformative opportunity. However, this opportunity didn't unfold in conventional fashion. Some may argue that the stars aligned in an improbable manner, making this story appear almost unbelievable. But I'll leave that judgment to you.

In the introduction of this book, it's important to establish the authenticity of the narrative. Thus, we begin by acknowledging that while the story is based on the real-life experiences of Keith Henderson, for the sake of narrative clarity and privacy, the protagonist's name has been replaced with that of a longtime friend, Michael. This adjustment allows us to delve into the compelling journey of personal growth and financial transformation without compromising the integrity of the account. Through Michael's journey, readers will glean invaluable insights and practical lessons that can empower them to navigate their own path to financial success and fulfillment.

But before we delve into the details of this transformative journey, I want to take a moment to share with you a guiding principle that has shaped my life for more than 25 years.

Since high school, I've lived by a famous quote—a mantra that has served as a source of inspiration and motivation through both rough times and good times. This quote was ingrained in me by my high school football coach, who would make the team members recite it each day before practice to ignite our spirits and fuel our determination. The words of wisdom came from none other than "Coach Hurt," one of our esteemed football coaches, whose influence extended far beyond the gridiron.

The quote goes as follows:

"This is the beginning of a new day. God has given us this day to use as we will. We can waste it or use it for good. For what we do today is important, for we are exchanging a day of our lives for it. We want it to be good, not bad; gain, not loss; success, not failure, in order that we never regret the price that we paid for it."

These profound words encapsulate the essence of seizing the opportunities that each day presents us with. They remind us that every moment is precious, and that it is up to us to make the most of the time we've been given. Whether we choose to waste it or use it for good, the decisions we make today have the power to shape our future and determine our success.

As I embarked on my journey from a 12-hour job to a lucrative opportunity, these words echoed in my mind, guiding me through the challenges and uncertainties that lay ahead. They reminded me of the importance of seizing every opportunity for growth and advancement, and of the power of determination and perseverance in the face of adversity. And so, armed with the wisdom imparted to me by Coach Hurt and fueled by the desire to make the most of each day, I set out on a journey that would ultimately lead me to financial freedom and success beyond my wildest dreams. Join me as we explore the keys to unlocking the millionaire lurking inside you and discover how you too can turn your dreams into reality.

Let's Begin!

The Beginning

A few years ago, I was like many hardworking everyday individuals, putting in long hours to make ends meet and dreaming of a brighter future. Little did I know one simple question would alter the course of my life forever.

The purpose of this book is to shift the mind, inspire, and empower anyone working a regular job to seize the opportunity for financial transformation. Whether you're punching a clock, working the night shift, or grinding away in pursuit of your goals, I want you to know that becoming a millionaire is within your reach and never too late. You must think like the successful do. Take Warren Buffet for an example, he became a millionaire by the age of 30 but his true wealth came in his later years in life. It doesn't matter the age but starting will lead you to a road of happiness and financial prosperity.

Through a combination of increasing your current income and embracing a frugal lifestyle for a period of time, you can unlock the doors to financial freedom and create the life you've always dreamed of. Unlocking the millionaire inside is not an easy task. It's also not as difficult to achieve but once you start thinking as the millionaires do and doing as the millionaires do, you'll soon understand how to unlock your true potential.

In the following pages, I will share with you an impactful story and the keys to financial success that I've discovered on my own journey. From disciplined debt paying, saving, different investment strategies to strategic decision-making, each chapter is designed to provide you with practical insights and actionable steps to help you unlock your mind to achieve millionaire status. But more than just offering advice, I'll take you behind the scenes of my own experiences, sharing the highs, lows, and invaluable lessons learned along the way.

As you embark on this journey with me, I encourage you to approach it with an open mind and a willingness to take action. While the path to becoming a millionaire may not always be easy, I passionately believe that with dedication, perseverance, and the right mindset, you can overcome any obstacle and achieve your wildest dreams. So, let's dive in together and unlock the millionaire that lies within each and every one of us.

Now Get Serious

To trigger the unlocking mechanism in your mind, you must adopt a serious mindset. Getting serious about your future is the cornerstone of achieving financial success and securing a prosperous life. It involves meticulously planning the trajectory of your life over the next 5 to 10 years, envisioning where you want to be, what you aspire to accomplish, and how you aim to live. By taking proactive steps to map out your future, you inherently shift your mindset towards one of intentionality, purpose, and determination. This process of serious contemplation and strategic planning empowers you to identify your long-term goals and aspirations, allowing you to chart a clear path towards their realization. Whether it's attaining financial independence, advancing in your career, starting a business, or achieving personal fulfillment, getting serious about your future provides you with the clarity and direction necessary to turn your dreams into tangible realities.

Moreover, this deliberate approach instills a sense of accountability and responsibility, compelling you to take decisive action towards your goals. It prompts you to make informed decisions, prioritize your time and resources, and cultivate the habits and behaviors conducive to success. By embracing this mindset of seriousness and commitment, you position yourself to overcome obstacles, navigate challenges, and stay focused on your journey towards a brighter future. Ultimately, getting serious about your future is not merely about setting lofty aspirations, but about taking deliberate and consistent steps to bring them to fruition. It requires discipline, resilience, and unwavering dedication to your vision, even in the face of adversity. By embracing this mindset and actively shaping your destiny, you empower yourself to create the life you desire and deserve.

Chapter I: Step Outside of the Box

Michael's journey towards success began early in life, as he demonstrated natural leadership qualities and a strong work ethic from a young age. Even as a child, Michael stood out as a leader, guiding his peewee football team to three championships, and earning recognition as a standout player on multiple occasions. As Michael moved on to junior high school, his determination and leadership on the field caught the attention of coaches, paving the way for opportunities to practice with the high school team while still in junior high.

Despite not being the biggest player on the field, Michael's sheer determination and passion for the game set him apart. Coaches and teammates alike admired his work ethic and unwavering commitment to excellence and his leadership. This pattern of success continued into high school, where Michael continued to excel both academically and athletically.

In addition to his achievements on the football field, Michael displayed a remarkable ability to succeed in other areas of his life. While attending high school, he balanced his studies with a full-time job at McDonald's, quickly rising through the ranks to become a crew leader. Michael's dedication and leadership skills were evident in his role at the fast-food restaurant, where he effectively managed operations and motivated his team to deliver exceptional service.

Despite facing financial challenges at home, Michael remained resilient and focused on his goals. His parents worked tirelessly to provide for their family, instilling in Michael a strong work ethic and a determination to succeed. Unaware of his parents' struggles, Michael sought out additional opportunities to earn money through side hustles, demonstrating his resourcefulness and entrepreneurial spirit.

Michael excelled on the football field collecting several MVP awards. Michael was sure to move on to the collegiate level but his mother's love and worries, talked Michael out of pursuing his dream to becoming an NFL football star. During Michael's last year of high school, Michael suffered an arm injury but kept playing throughout the year through pain and suffering. Michael visited with many college recruiters, but his mind was consumed by his mother's words and thoughts of his son being injured permanently. After high school, Michael immediately went into surgery to prepare his injured arm and would miss his first year of college. While at home for the summer following his high school graduation, Michael sat with his arm in a cast and thought about his future.

Michael then got up and started searching for new jobs so he could make more money to support himself and family as he neared removing the cast and starting rehabilitation. Michael ended up receiving a phone call for an interview, but he was worried about getting the job due to the cast being on his arm. Michael still went to the interview and was able to land the job. During the interview, Michael explained what happened to his arm and mentioned to the interviewer that it was temporary, and he could perform the job as soon as the cast came off within a few weeks. 2-3 months later, Michael was working well and thinking about when he could get back on the football field for the next college season. But fate had other plans. Michael's father lost his job due to a shutdown. Michael did the only thing a good son would do. He stepped in and provided support to his family and put his dreams on hold. Michael never played another day of football.

Michael continued to thrive in the workforce, securing the position with a local technology company. His exemplary performance caught the attention of company leadership, and he was quickly promoted to a shift lead role. Once again, Michael's leadership skills shone through as he inspired his team to achieve new levels of success and productivity.

Throughout his journey, Michael's unwavering determination, strong work ethic, and natural leadership abilities propelled him forward, allowing him to overcome obstacles and achieve his goals. From the football field to the workplace, Michael's commitment to excellence and his ability to lead by example set him apart as a true success story.

As Michael continued to settle into his new shift lead role at work, he began to reap the rewards of his hard work and dedication in the form of extra pay. With this newfound increase Michael started to contemplate the idea of moving out of his parents' home and into his own place. His father was able to land a higher paying job as a mechanic, so Michael felt it was time for him to step aside and give the reigns of leading the family back to his father.

Seeking guidance from his father, Michael discussed his options for housing and whether it would be wise to rent an apartment on his own or consider living with a friend to help share expenses. His father, drawing from his own experiences and wisdom, offered Michael valuable advice about the benefits of homeownership.

While Michael initially considered the idea of buying a home to be daunting and out of reach, his father shared insights into the long-term advantages of investing in property. Although Michael didn't fully grasp the concept at the time, his father's words planted a seed of curiosity and interest in the potential benefits of homeownership.

Despite his initial reservations, Michael began to see homeownership not just as a place to live, but as a strategic financial move that could positively impact his future. The idea of building equity and investing in his own future appealed to Michael's entrepreneurial spirit and desire for financial independence.

Although he didn't fully understand the intricacies of buying a home at the time, Michael trusted in his father's wisdom and began to explore the possibility further.

Michael's decision-making process regarding housing was heavily influenced by his father and his close friend, Alonzo. When Michael contemplated moving out from his childhood home and venturing into independent living, his father emphasized deeply the importance of buying a home instead of renting an apartment. Understanding the long-term benefits of homeownership, Michael's father urged him to consider investing in a property that would appreciate over time, rather than wasting money on rent.

Meanwhile, Michael found an unexpected source of inspiration in his coworker, Alonzo. As they forged a friendship and would eventually become true brothers, Michael observed Alonzo's journey towards purchasing his own home. Alonzo's dedication to homeownership and his diligent approach to financial planning left a lasting impression on

Michael. He admired Alonzo's commitment to building equity and creating a stable foundation for his future.

Although initially uncertain about the significance of buying a home, Michael's interactions with both his father and Alonzo sparked a shift in his perspective. He began to see homeownership not just as a financial investment, but as a symbol of stability, security, and personal accomplishment. Guided by the wisdom of his father and inspired by the example set by Alonzo, Michael made the decision to pursue homeownership as a milestone in his journey towards financial independence.

In this way, the influence of both his father and his friend Alonzo played a pivotal role in shaping Michael's mindset and guiding his decisions as he embarked on a new chapter of his life. Their guidance and mentorship instilled in him a sense of purpose and determination to step outside the box and pursue opportunities that would lead to long-term success and fulfillment. Little did Michael know that this decision would set him on a path towards greater financial stability and success in the years to come.

After Michael settled into his new home, he found a sense of peace in his surroundings. However, as time passed, the daily struggles of life began to accumulate. Despite facing challenges and obstacles along the way, Michael remained resilient and steadfast in his determination to overcome adversity. Whether confronted with good times or hard times, Michael persevered, maintaining his focus, and pushing forward with unwavering resolve but Michael's life was a whirlwind of activity. From the moment he opened his eyes in the evening until he collapsed into bed early with the morning light, he was in perpetual motion, constantly juggling the demands of work, school, and family. The days blurred together as he navigated the hectic schedule of a man on a mission—a mission to make ends meet and continue his education against all odds.

Working the night shift from 6 pm to 6 am was grueling, but Michael was no stranger to hard work. He learned hard work and many trades from his father who was a mechanic and carpenter that could rebuild any car engine and look at any small structure and build it from memory. Michaels father always included him in many projects worked on at his childhood home. Michael shared many traits from his father. But one that was not like any other was special dreams. Michael and his father could dream about an issue or problem and the way to fix the issue would come in the form of a dream. This trait still holds true today. With each passing hour, Michael toiled away, his mind consumed with thoughts of the future and the promise of a better life. But it wasn't just work that filled his days. In between shifts, he squeezed in classes at the local college, determined to pursue his education and carve out a brighter future for himself and his loved ones.

Michael's early struggles as a young parent, striving to care for his son, Zyon, amidst challenging circumstances. With times proving exceedingly tough, Michael found solace in the unwavering support of his sister, Valerie, and his parents. Often, Michael faced hardships without asking for help, resorting to inventive measures to provide for his son. One such strategy involved collecting receipts from Burger King and scouring them for surveys on the back. These surveys offered the chance to redeem meals at half price upon completion, allowing Michael to stretch his meager budget and ensure both he and Zyon had sustenance for less than $2.00. Such resourcefulness epitomized Michael's determination to navigate adversity and carve out a better future for himself and his son.

Life was happening fast for Michael, and it felt like everything was falling apart. Bills piled up, deadlines loomed, and the weight of responsibility bore down on his shoulders. But amidst the chaos, there was a glimmer of hope—a chance encounter that would change everything.

It happened one day at the local car wash, where Michael found himself scrubbing away the grime of the city off his truck. As Michael finished washing his car at the carwash, wiping down the last few drops of water from a freshly washed car then moving on to the next station, he noticed a sleek BMW M3 pull up behind his truck. Terry, the owner of the BMW, seemed to be having trouble accessing the vacuum cleaners due to the length of Michael's truck bed. Sensing the need to assist, Michael quietly climbed into his truck and maneuvered it forward, giving Terry enough space to reach the vacuums.

Terry, a gregarious New Yorker with a flair for conversation, didn't say anything at the time. Michael couldn't help but compliment Terry on his impressive car, breaking the ice with a simple remark. Terry immediately struck up a chat with Michael. His eyes gleamed with pride as he talked about one of his eight prized vehicles the SMG BMW shimmering in the sunlight. Michael, usually a quiet and reserved individual, found himself drawn into Terry's charismatic energy. Terry was unlike anyone Michael had ever met before. Charismatic and confident, he exuded an aura of possibility—a sense that there was more to life than the daily grind.

The conversation flowed effortlessly between the two men as they exchanged pleasantries and anecdotes. Terry's animated storytelling and infectious laughter brought a rare warmth to the otherwise mundane surroundings of the carwash. Despite his initial inclination to keep to himself, Michael found himself enjoying the company and camaraderie. As the conversation meandered on, Michael's curiosity piqued, and he couldn't resist the urge to inquire about Terry's occupation. With a casual yet genuine interest, Michael asked Terry what he did for a living.

Terry shared glimpses of his own journey—a journey that had taken him far beyond the confines of their small town and into the heart of a war-torn country halfway across the world. Iraq! Terry asked Michael what he did for a living and Michael went on to explain his job, hours, and days he worked. Terry replied, ahh yes, we have people doing those jobs overseas. With each word Terry spoke, Michael felt a stirring deep within him—a restless longing for something more, something greater than the monotony of his current existence.

And then, like a bolt from the blue, Terry made him an offer—a chance to step outside the box, to venture into the unknown, to journey to a place where danger and opportunity coexisted in equal measure. Michael was thinking! It was a leap of faith unlike any other, a decision that would irrevocably alter the course of Michael's life. And so, with a mixture of trepidation and excitement coursing through his veins, Michael said yes, "please let me know what I need to do". Terry said, don't worry, I can help you!

Terry and Michael exchanged contact information and they both parted ways. As Michael pulled away little did he know, that this one seemingly ordinary encounter with a total stranger would become the turning point in his life. As he mustered the courage to engage in conversation with Terry, a man he had never met before, little did he realize that his curiosity would unlock the door to a world of possibilities he had never imagined. With just one simple question, Michael unwittingly set in motion a chain of events that would propel him towards a destiny far beyond the confines of his everyday routine.

Months passed, and Michael found himself consumed with thoughts of the future. He had been in regular contact with Terry but then the dreams began to fade. No new job, conversations with Terry had slowed and Michael forgot about the conversation and opportunity and got back to his regular life. Then, one fateful day in February, Michael found himself seated at his desk, his mind consumed by the early evening myriad tasks. Suddenly, he veered off course, his attention drawn to the cluttered chaos of his email inbox. Without any particular reason driving him, he impulsively decided to tackle the disarray, starting with a sweep through his primary inbox and then his spam folder. Yet, as his eyes darted across the screen in a swift motion, time seemed to halt, his focus captured by an unfamiliar name: Ivy Jane Caasey. Unbeknownst to him, the contents of that email held the potential to completely reshape his future.

The email was from a company recruiter, buried amidst a sea of junk mail. It was dated a month prior—an oversight that sent his heart racing. Without a moment's hesitation, Michael dashed to the conference room, where he could make a private phone call.

As Michael dialed the number to the recruiter, a whirlwind of doubts swirled in his mind. Was it too late in the evening? Would the recruiter be in the office at this time? Would it be too late? Had they already filled the position? Would they even answer the phone, or was it all just an information junk email? But as the phone rang on, each uncertain thought intensified. Then, suddenly, a soft and polite voice greeted him with a simple "Hello." It was Ivey Jane Caasey who had answered. As Michael conversed with Ms. Cassey, he couldn't help but mention the peculiar circumstance surrounding their communication. "I actually found your email in my spam folder," he admitted, somewhat sheepishly. However, to his relief, the recruiter responded with understanding. "Ah, yes, we've been trying to reach you," she acknowledged. "But no worries, I'm glad you contacted us back." With that simple reassurance, Michael felt a weight lift from his shoulders, grateful for the chance to finally connect and move forward with the opportunity at hand.

The conversation with the recruiter was nothing short of miraculous. Michael engaged in a brief discussion about the job duties and was asked if he could perform them. Without hesitation, Michael confidently affirmed his capability and proceeded to articulate his reasons why and how he could fulfill the responsibilities. And with that, the interview concluded. She explained that they had been trying to reach him for weeks, eager to offer him a once-in-a-lifetime opportunity to work in Iraq for 4 times the amount his current salary. It was as if fate had intervened, paving the way for Michael to take the next step on his journey to financial freedom and success. The recruiter had one final question for Michael. Ms. Cassey asked, would you like to accept this offer? Michael's eyes grew, and immediately yelled out YES! Michael accepted the offer over the phone at that precise time and once the phone call ended, he sat in disbelief in that conference room and cried. Michael's decision to accept the job offer in Iraq wasn't just a personal milestone—it was a seismic shift that would impact his entire family. 1 week later, Michael received the official offer letter and documents for the job.

As he prepared to embark on this new chapter of his life, he knew that he would have to have a difficult conversation with his parents about the dangers of his chosen path. Michael first contacted his sister Valerie, and she gave Michael full support as she always did. Michael's sister was a strong woman and, on many occasions, had helped Michael through many financial issues, trials, and tribulations. After the discussion with his sister. Michael was able to build the nerves to speak with his loving mother and father. Sitting them down one evening, Michael braced himself for their reaction, knowing full well that his mother, in particular, would struggle to see beyond the risks just as she did to detour him from playing football.

Michael's father supported him but there were some doubts about the dangers, but Michael's father knew the type of son he had shaped and formed to be able to do anything in this life. His mother's initial reaction was one of disbelief and fear. She couldn't fathom why her son would willingly put himself in harm's way, venturing into battle-scarred territories thousands of miles from home. Tears welled up in her eyes as she pleaded with Michael to reconsider, to choose a safer, more conventional path. But Michael knew that he couldn't turn back this time—he had to follow his instincts, no matter the cost.

With a heavy heart, Michael looked his mother in the eye and uttered words that he knew would break her heart. "Mom," he said gently, "I have to do this. I know it's risky, but I believe it's the right decision for me." His voice trembled with emotion as he spoke, his resolve unwavering in the face of uncertainty. "If I don't make it out of Iraq," he continued, his voice faltering slightly, "please know that I tried my best. I tried to make a difference, to build a better future for myself and for our family."

For Michael, the conversation with his parents was a defining moment—a test of his convictions and his ability to stand firm in the face of opposition. Despite his mother's fears and reservations, he remained steadfast in his belief that this was the path he was meant to take. And as he looked into her eyes, he saw a glimmer of understanding amidst the tears—a silent acknowledgment of his courage and determination.

In the days leading up to his departure, Michael cherished every moment with his family, knowing that it might be the last time he saw them. He hugged his mother tightly, whispering words of reassurance and love as she clung to him, her heart heavy with worry. And as he said his final goodbyes, he carried with him the weight of their hopes and fears, their love, and their prayers, knowing that they would be his guiding light in the days ahead. Michael also sat down with his young son Zyon and nephew Malik. Both, too young to understand what he was about to do. Both Zyon and Malik were cheerful young boys and were always smiling and simply happy to see their father and uncle. With tears in Michael's eyes, he told them he had to go away for a little while, but he'd call to talk and to make sure they were always doing ok. They really didn't understand but Michael had to tell them anyway to clear his heart.

And so, with a newfound sense of purpose and determination, Michael embarked on the adventure of a lifetime, leaving behind the familiar comforts of home in pursuit of a brighter future.

Before Michael's departure for Iraq, he had to undergo a rigorous readiness training at the CRC (CONUS Replacement Center). This training served as a vital preparation for the challenges that lay ahead, both in terms of the cultural nuances of Iraq and the inherent dangers of living and working in a war zone. As he immersed himself in the training, Michael couldn't help but feel a sense of trepidation about the journey he was about to embark on. The reality of what he had signed up for was beginning to sink in, and he couldn't help but wonder what he had gotten himself into.

Despite his apprehension, Michael's resolve remained unshaken. He recalled the words he had spoken to his mother before leaving words that served as a silent mantra during moments of doubt and uncertainty. "If I don't make it," he had told her, "At least I tried." It was a reminder to himself that even in the face of adversity, he was determined to give it his all, to seize every opportunity that came his way, and to never look back with regret.

The CRC training provided Michael with invaluable insights into the cultural and logistical challenges he would encounter upon his arrival in Iraq. From language lessons to survival skills, he absorbed as much information as he could, eager to equip himself with the tools necessary to navigate the unfamiliar terrain that awaited him. Yet, despite the thorough preparation, there was no denying the gravity of the situation. The dangers were real, and the stakes were high.

As Michael underwent the final preparations for his departure, he couldn't shake the feeling of uncertainty that lingered in the back of his mind. What if he wasn't ready? What if he couldn't handle the challenges that lay ahead? These doubts gnawed at him, threatening to undermine his confidence. But then he remembered his father and mother's words— the words of encouragement and support that had propelled him forward in the face of uncertainty.

With a renewed sense of determination, Michael boarded the plane bound for Kuwait, ready to face whatever challenges lay ahead. He knew that the road ahead would be fraught with obstacles and uncertainties, but he was determined to persevere. For he knew that this was just the beginning of his journey— Little did he know that this leap of faith outside of this small window he had been looking out of his entire life, would be the catalyst for a series of events that would ultimately lead him to the keys of financial success and the fulfillment of his deepest dreams. Michael braced himself for whatever lay ahead, knowing that he had the love and support of his family guiding him every step of the way.

Michael's journey overseas began with a stark introduction to the harsh realities of the Middle Eastern climate. Touching down in Kuwait on July 4th, he was immediately met with a wave of intense heat that enveloped him like a blast from an oven. The sweltering 120-degree Fahrenheit temperature was a stark reminder that he was far from the familiar comforts of home.

However, Michael's arrival in Kuwait marked just the beginning of his trials. Stranded for three months due to visa clearance issues, he found himself in a state of limbo, unsure of when he would be able to proceed to his final destination in Iraq. Despite the frustration of the delay, Michael recognized it as an opportunity to immerse himself in a new culture. While his company paid him a small base salary for essentially doing nothing, he took advantage of the time to explore Kuwait, sampling its cuisine, and learning about its rich history.

After what felt like an eternity, Michael finally received clearance to proceed to Baghdad International Airport, or BIAP. Yet, the living conditions upon his arrival were far from ideal. Housed in what was once Saddam Hussein's son's zoo, the makeshift living quarters were a far cry from the comforts of home. Michael found himself residing in a place ominously dubbed "Plywood Palace." Despite its regal-sounding name, the reality was harsh. Constructed entirely from plywood and 2x4s, the cramped living quarters offered little respite from the harsh desert climate.

Sharing a small room measuring just 8 feet by 10 feet with another person, Michael quickly realized that adaptability would be key to surviving in this unforgiving environment. And if the stifling heat and cramped living quarters weren't challenging enough, the presence of oversized mosquitoes added an extra layer of discomfort. Their tiger-striped bodies were a constant reminder of the dangers lurking just beyond the confines of their makeshift shelter.

But despite the hardships he faced, Michael remained determined to persevere. He knew that this was just the beginning of his journey—a test of his resilience and determination in the face of adversity. And as he looked out at the horizon, he knew that it was time to embrace change—to adapt to his new surroundings and make the best of the situation.

In the weeks and months that followed, Michael found himself gradually acclimating to his new environment. He forged friendships with his fellow coworkers, bonding over shared experiences and facing challenges together as a team. And with each passing day, he gained a deeper understanding of the complexities of life in a conflict zone—a perspective that would shape his worldview in ways he never could have imagined. Despite the hardships he faced, Michael approached each day with a sense of optimism and determination. Trying desperately to adapt he refused to let the hardships and setbacks define him, instead viewing them as opportunities for growth and self-discovery. And as he settled into his new routine, he began to appreciate the beauty and resilience of the human spirit—the unwavering resolve that allows us to endure even the darkest of times.

Looking back on those early days in Kuwait and Baghdad, Michael couldn't help but marvel at how far he had come. What had once seemed insurmountable had now become a testament to his resilience and determination. And as he gazed out at the horizon, he remembered what was told to him by an old friend. You cannot stay in environments where people don't know the true value of you. Michael knew that the journey was far from over.

Key Points to unlocking your mindset

For everyday working people to change their mindset and leave their comfort zone, here are some key points.

I. Recognize the Status Quo: Understand that staying in your comfort zone may feel safe, but it can also limit your growth and potential. Recognize that change is necessary for progress and success.

2. Define Your Goals: Take the time to define your goals and aspirations. What do you want to achieve in your career, finances, and personal life? Having clear goals will provide direction and motivation to step outside your comfort zone.

3. Challenge Limiting Beliefs: Identify and challenge any limiting beliefs or negative self-talk that may be holding you back. Replace these with positive affirmations and a growth mindset that embraces challenges and opportunities.

4. Embrace Fear: Understand that fear is a natural response to stepping outside your comfort zone. Instead of letting fear paralyze you, embrace it as a sign that you are pushing yourself to grow and evolve.

5. Take Small Steps: Break down your goals into smaller, manageable steps. Start by taking small actions outside your comfort zone each day. Gradually increase the level of challenge as you build confidence and momentum.

6. Seek Support: Surround yourself with supportive individuals who encourage and inspire you to push your boundaries. Seek out mentors, coaches, or peers who have successfully navigated similar challenges.

7. Focus on Growth: Shift your focus from perfection to progress. Understand that growth and learning often involve making mistakes and facing setbacks. Embrace these as opportunities to learn and grow stronger.

8. Visualize Success: Visualize yourself succeeding in your endeavors. Use visualization techniques to imagine yourself stepping confidently outside your comfort zone and achieving your goals.

9. Celebrate Achievements: Celebrate your successes, no matter how small. Acknowledge and reward yourself for stepping outside your comfort zone and taking proactive steps towards your goals.

10. Stay Persistent: Understand that leaving your comfort zone is a journey, not a destination. Stay persistent and resilient in the face of challenges and setbacks. Remember that each step forward brings you closer to unlocking your million-dollar mindset.

Let Michael's journey serve as a beacon of inspiration, urging us all to step outside of the box when pursuing our dreams and aspirations. His resilience in the face of adversity, his innovative solutions to life's challenges, and his unwavering determination to create a better future for himself and his loved ones are testament to the transformative power of thinking outside conventional boundaries. As you embark on your own path, remember that greatness often lies beyond the confines of the familiar. Embrace uncertainty, challenge the status quo, and dare to defy expectations. By stepping outside of the box, you open yourself to endless possibilities and unlock the potential to achieve extraordinary feats. So, let Michael's story ignite the spark of courage within you, propelling you towards the realization of your boldest dreams.

Chapter 2: Embracing Change

As Michael settled into his new life in Iraq, he quickly realized that embracing change was not just a necessity—it was a mindset. The opportunity to work in a foreign country brought with it a wealth of new experiences, challenges, and perspectives. One of the most transformative aspects of this journey was the opportunity to meet people from all walks of life, each with their own unique views and ideas. Interacting with individuals from diverse backgrounds broadened Michael's horizons and challenged his preconceived notions. Whether it was sharing stories over meals in the makeshift mess hall or engaging in lively debates during downtime, he found himself constantly learning and growing. These interactions fostered a spirit of curiosity and open-mindedness, encouraging Michael to embrace new ways of thinking and approaching problems.

One of the most profound experiences for Michael was speaking to different military personnel stationed in Iraq. These brave men and women risked their lives every day in service to their country, embodying the values of courage, sacrifice, and selflessness. Their stories of resilience and determination served as a constant reminder of the importance of perseverance in the face of adversity. Among the countless individuals Michael encountered during his time in Iraq, there were a few who stood out as mentors—retired military personnel with a wealth of knowledge and experience to share. These mentors became invaluable guides, offering insights and advice gleaned from years of service in the armed forces. Their wisdom and guidance helped Michael navigate the complexities of life in a war zone and provided him with invaluable information and lessons that would shape his journey moving forward.

The decision to accept the job offer in Iraq was not one that Michael took lightly. It was a leap of faith—a bold step into the unknown that would ultimately shape the trajectory of his life. Yet, despite the uncertainties and risks involved, Michael knew deep down that it was the right decision for him.

The impact of this decision on Michael's financial trajectory was profound. It represented a turning point—a pivotal moment in which he seized the opportunity for growth and advancement. By stepping outside of his comfort zone and embracing the challenges that lay ahead, Michael set himself on a path towards financial stability and success.

The journey was not without its challenges, of course. There were moments of doubt and uncertainty, times when Michael questioned whether he had made the right choice. But with each obstacle he faced, he emerged stronger and more resilient, fortified by the knowledge that he was capable of overcoming any challenge that came his way.

As Michael settled into his role as a network VSAT engineer, he quickly realized that success in this new endeavor would require him to learn new skills and adapt to unfamiliar tasks. One of the most challenging aspects of the job was working in the scorching heat of the Iraqi desert, where temperatures soared to a blistering 120 degrees Fahrenheit. Despite the harsh conditions, Michael knew that he had to persevere if he wanted to succeed.

One of the tasks that Michael found himself tackling was drilling holes in the concrete pavements to install fiber ramps. These ramps were essential for allowing cabling to cross the street safely, ensuring that communication networks remained operational in the face of many challenges. It was grueling work, requiring precision and attention to detail, but Michael approached it with determination and a willingness to learn.

Learning new skills on the job was not easy for Michael. It required patience, perseverance, and a willingness to step outside of his comfort zone. But with each passing day, he found himself growing more confident in his abilities and more adept at tackling the challenges that came his way. And as he honed his skills, he began to see the fruits of his labor, making tangible contributions to the success of the mission. Despite the obstacles he faced, Michael remained undeterred in his pursuit of excellence. He sought out opportunities for growth and development, eager to expand his knowledge and expertise in the field of network infrastructure, and with the support of his colleagues and mentors, he was able to overcome the initial hurdles and excel in his role.

As he reflected on his journey, Michael realized that embracing change meant more than just adapting to new circumstances—it meant embracing the opportunity for growth and self-improvement. It meant pushing past the limits of what he thought was possible and challenging himself to reach new heights. And in doing so, he discovered a newfound sense of confidence and purpose that would propel him forward on his journey towards success.

Michael's willingness to learn new skills and adapt to new challenges was a testament to his resilience and determination. It was a journey of self-discovery and personal growth—a journey that ultimately led him to overcome obstacles and to achieve one of many goals of adapting and accepting change. And as he looked towards the future, he knew that there would be many more challenges ahead, but he was ready to face them head-on, armed with the knowledge that he had the skills and the determination to succeed.

Looking back on his journey, Michael realized that embracing change was not just about seizing opportunities—it was about embracing the unknown, facing adversity head-on, and emerging stronger on the other side. It was about recognizing that growth and advancement often lie on the other side of discomfort and uncertainty and having the courage to step boldly into the unknown. In the end, Michael's decision to embrace change was one that would shape the course of his life in ways he never could have imagined. It was a journey of self-discovery, resilience, and growth—a journey that ultimately led him to the fulfillment of his dreams and the realization of his true potential. And as he looked towards the future, Michael knew that the best was yet to come.

Key points for embracing change

1. Acceptance: Understand that change is an inevitable part of life. Instead of resisting it, practice acceptance and acknowledge that change can lead to growth and new opportunities.

2. Positive Outlook: Cultivate a positive mindset towards change. Rather than viewing it as a threat, see it as a chance for personal and professional development. Focus on the potential benefits and opportunities that change can bring.

3. Flexibility: Be flexible and adaptable in the face of change. Embrace the unknown and be open to new experiences and possibilities. Flexibility allows you to navigate change more effectively and with less stress.

4. Learning Opportunity: Approach change as a learning opportunity. Each change brings valuable lessons and insights that can help you grow and evolve as an individual. Embrace the opportunity to learn and expand your knowledge and skills.

5. Resilience: Develop resilience to bounce back from setbacks and challenges that may accompany change. Understand that setbacks are a natural part of the change process and use them as opportunities for growth and self-improvement.

6. Embrace Uncertainty: Learn to embrace uncertainty and ambiguity. Understand that change often involves stepping into the unknown and be willing to take calculated risks. Embracing uncertainty can lead to new discoveries and breakthroughs.

7. Seek Support: Surround yourself with a supportive network of friends, family, colleagues, and mentors who can provide guidance and encouragement during times of change. Lean on them for support and advice as you navigate through transitions.

8. Focus on Solutions: Instead of dwelling on problems or challenges that may arise from change, focus on finding solutions and taking proactive steps forward. Approach changes with a problem-solving mindset and look for opportunities to innovate and adapt.

9. Celebrate Progress: Celebrate small wins and milestones along the way. Recognize and acknowledge your progress, no matter how small, as you navigate through change. Celebrating progress boosts morale and motivation, keeping you focused on your goals.

10. Persistence: Stay persistent and resilient in the face of change. Understand that change may not always happen overnight and may require time, effort, and perseverance. Keep moving forward, even in the face of obstacles, and never give up on your goals and aspirations.

Financial Key points of acceptance of change with newfound income

Here are steps to embrace financial changes for the better and stay frugal while living within your means if you find extra money or side jobs to help you along the way.

1. Assess Your Financial Situation: Start by evaluating your current financial situation. Take stock of your income, expenses, debts, and savings. Understanding where you stand financially will help you identify areas for improvement.

2. Set Financial Goals: Define clear and achievable financial goals that align with your values and priorities. Whether it's paying off debt, building an emergency fund, saving for retirement, or purchasing a home, having specific goals will provide direction and motivation.

3. Create a Budget: Develop a realistic budget that outlines your income and expenses. Allocate your funds to cover essential expenses such as housing, utilities, groceries, and transportation, while also setting aside money for savings and debt repayment. Track your spending regularly to ensure you stay within your budget.

4. Prioritize Saving: Make saving a priority by setting aside a portion of your income each month. Aim to save at least 10% of your earnings, if possible, for emergencies and future financial goals. Set up automatic transfers to a savings account to make saving effortless.

5. Live Below Your Means: Resist the temptation to overspend and live beyond your means. Avoid unnecessary purchases and prioritize needs over wants. Embrace a minimalist lifestyle by focusing on experiences and relationships rather than material possessions.

6. Track Your Expenses: Keep track of your expenses to identify areas where you can cut back and save money. Look for opportunities to reduce discretionary spending on non-essential items such as dining out, entertainment, and subscription services.

7. Practice Frugality: Embrace frugality by finding ways to save money on everyday expenses. Shop for deals, use coupons, buy generic brands, and look for opportunities to save on utilities and other recurring bills. Adopting frugal habits can help stretch your dollars further and increase your savings over time.

8. Avoid Debt: Minimize debt by avoiding unnecessary borrowing and living within your means. Pay off high-interest debt as quickly as possible and avoid using credit cards for purchases you can't afford to pay off in full each month. Prioritize debt repayment to free up more money for savings and investments.

9. Invest Wisely: Educate yourself about different investment options and consider investing in assets that offer long-term growth potential, such as stocks, bonds, mutual funds, and real estate. Start small and gradually increase your investments over time as you become more comfortable with the process.

10. Review and Adjust: Regularly review your financial situation and adjust your strategies as needed. Monitor your progress towards your goals, track your spending habits, and make changes to your budget and savings plan as necessary. Stay disciplined and committed to your financial journey, knowing that small changes can lead to significant long-term benefits.

Chapter 2 serves as a beacon, shedding light on the critical importance of embracing change as we navigate the winding path towards financial freedom and a more fulfilling life. It underscores the undeniable truth that change is an integral part of our existence, presenting us with both challenges and opportunities along the way. For the everyday working individual, recognizing the inevitability of change and understanding its transformative potential is paramount.

Change, far from being a force to be feared or resisted, is in fact a catalyst for growth, innovation, and progress. It is through change that we are compelled to reassess our circumstances, reevaluate our goals, and adapt our strategies accordingly. By embracing change with an open mind and a resilient spirit, we can transform obstacles into steppingstones, turning adversity into advantage, and paving the way towards a brighter future.

In the face of change, we must not succumb to fear or hesitation, but rather, we must seize the moment and leverage it as an opportunity for personal and financial advancement. It is through our willingness to embrace change that we can pivot our paths towards success, unlocking the doors to financial freedom and realizing our true potential.

So, let us embrace change wholeheartedly, for within its embrace lies the power to manifest our dreams and aspirations. Let us greet each new challenge with courage and determination, knowing that it is through overcoming adversity that we grow stronger and wiser. Together, let us embark on this journey of transformation, confident in our ability to navigate the ever-changing currents of life and emerge victorious on the other side.

Chapter 3: Unlock The Mind of Mastering Financial Intelligence

Financial intelligence encompasses the ability to effectively manage one's finances, make informed decisions, and navigate the complexities of the financial world. At its core, it involves understanding key concepts such as income, expenses, assets, and liabilities, and how they interplay to shape one's financial well-being. Income refers to the money earned or received, typically through employment, investments, or other sources. It is the primary source of funds that individuals use to meet their financial needs and goals. Understanding the nature and amount of one's income is crucial for budgeting, planning, and achieving financial stability. Expenses, on the other hand, encompass the money spent or paid out to cover various costs and obligations.

These may include rent or mortgage payments, utility bills, groceries, transportation, entertainment, debt repayments, and more. Managing expenses effectively involves tracking spending, prioritizing needs over wants, and finding ways to reduce unnecessary costs. The difference between income and expenses forms the basis of financial health and stability. Ideally, individuals should aim to maintain a positive cash flow, where income exceeds expenses. This surplus can then be allocated towards savings, investments, debt repayment, and other financial goals, helping to build wealth over time. Assets are resources or possessions owned by an individual that have economic value and can generate income or appreciate in value over time.

Examples include real estate, stocks, bonds, retirement accounts, business ownership, and valuable possessions like vehicles and jewelry. Assets contribute to one's net worth and provide avenues for wealth accumulation and financial security. Liabilities, on the other hand, represent financial obligations or debts owed by an individual to creditors or lenders. This may include mortgages, car loans, student loans, credit card debt, and other forms of borrowing. Unlike assets, liabilities detract from one's net worth and can impose financial burdens through interest payments and repayment obligations.

Financial intelligence involves understanding the relationship between assets and liabilities and making strategic decisions to leverage assets while minimizing liabilities. This may include prioritizing investments in income-generating assets, such as real estate or stocks, while minimizing debt and avoiding high-interest liabilities. By cultivating financial intelligence and mastering concepts such as income, expenses, assets, and liabilities, individuals can make informed financial decisions, build wealth, and achieve long-term financial security and independence.

The Money Trap

Many individuals fall into the trap of using their income to cover immediate expenses and liabilities, without allocating any funds towards building wealth. However, this approach ultimately hinders their financial progress and prevents them from achieving long-term prosperity. The key to unlocking financial wealth lies in breaking free from this cycle and adopting a more strategic approach to money management. Instead of simply spending their income on consumable goods and liabilities, individuals must prioritize investing in income-generating assets. These assets have the potential to generate returns and grow in value over time, thereby increasing one's overall wealth. By diverting a portion of their income towards investments, individuals can gradually build a portfolio of assets that will continue to generate passive income and appreciate in value.

Understanding this fundamental principle is essential for cultivating the mindset of a millionaire. Rather than focusing solely on immediate gratification, individuals must prioritize delayed gratification and invest in their future financial well-being. By consistently allocating funds towards income-generating assets and reinvesting the returns, individuals can accelerate their journey towards financial independence and wealth accumulation. This process of investing in assets and reinvesting the returns can be likened to a cycle that repeats itself over time.

As individuals continue to invest and reinvest, their wealth will gradually snowball, leading to exponential growth and prosperity. By delaying gratification in the short term, individuals can enjoy greater financial freedom and abundance in the long run. In essence, the key to unlocking the mindset of a millionaire lies in recognizing the importance of investing in assets that produce income and appreciating in value over time. By embracing delayed gratification and prioritizing wealth-building activities, individuals can set themselves on the path to financial success and achieve their long-term financial goals.

The Millionaire Mindset

Once individuals achieve millionaire status, their approach to money must fundamentally shifts. Rather than working solely to earn a paycheck, millionaires understand the power of making money work for them. This mindset shift marks a pivotal moment in their financial journey, where they transition from being laborers to investors and entrepreneurs. Millionaires recognize that traditional employment is just one of many avenues to generate income. Instead of relying solely on active income earned through employment, they focus on building multiple streams of passive income.

Passive income streams continue to generate money even when individuals are not actively working, allowing them to enjoy greater freedom and flexibility in how they use their time. One common way millionaires make money work for them is through investments. They deploy their capital into various asset classes such as stocks, bonds, real estate, and businesses, aiming to generate returns and grow their wealth over time. By diversifying their investment portfolio and leveraging compounding interest, they can create sustainable sources of passive income that continue to grow without requiring active involvement. Real estate investment is a popular choice among millionaires for generating passive income. They may purchase rental properties and collect monthly rental payments from tenants, allowing them to earn a steady stream of income while benefiting from property appreciation over time.

Additionally, some millionaires invest in real estate investment trusts (REITs) or crowdfunding platforms, which provide exposure to real estate assets without the need for direct property ownership. Another strategy employed by millionaires is to build and scale successful businesses. Rather than being directly involved in day-to-day operations, they may hire competent managers and employees to run the business, allowing them to step back and focus on strategic decision-making and expansion opportunities. Successful businesses can generate substantial profits and provide ongoing income streams for their owners. Additionally, millionaires may utilize financial instruments such as dividend-paying stocks, bonds, annuities, and royalties to generate passive income.

These investments provide regular payouts without requiring active participation, allowing millionaires to enjoy a steady stream of income while preserving their capital. Overall, the key principle behind making money work for you is to leverage your resources strategically, invest wisely, and build sustainable sources of passive income. By adopting this mindset and implementing sound financial strategies, millionaires can enjoy financial freedom and security, allowing them to live life on their own terms.

Asset Classes that individuals can acquire to build wealth and achieve financial freedom. Open your mind to these assets.

1. Real Estate: Rental properties, commercial real estate, or land investments can generate rental income and appreciate in value over time.

2. Stocks: Investing in stocks of publicly traded companies can provide capital appreciation and dividend income.

3. Bonds: Fixed-income securities such as government bonds or corporate bonds offer regular interest payments and return of principal upon maturity.

4. Mutual Funds: Diversified investment funds managed by professionals that pool money from multiple investors to invest in a variety of assets such as stocks, bonds, and commodities.

5. Exchange-Traded Funds (ETFs): Similar to mutual funds but traded on stock exchanges, ETFs offer diversification and flexibility with lower expense ratios.

6. Retirement Accounts: Contributing to retirement accounts like 401(k), IRA, or Roth IRA provides tax advantages and helps individuals save for retirement.

7. Business Ownership: Starting or investing in a business can generate profits and potential for growth, providing an additional income stream.

8. Intellectual Property: Patents, copyrights, trademarks, and royalties from creative works or inventions can generate passive income.

9. Precious Metals: Investing in gold, silver, or other precious metals can serve as a hedge against inflation and economic uncertainty.

10. Cryptocurrencies: Digital currencies like Bitcoin and Ethereum offer opportunities for capital appreciation but come with higher volatility and risk.

11. Peer-to-Peer Lending: Investing in peer-to-peer lending platforms allows individuals to earn interest by lending money directly to borrowers.

12. Collectibles: Rare coins, art, antiques, or collectible items can appreciate in value over time and serve as alternative investments.

13. Annuities: Insurance products that provide regular payments over a specified period or for life, offering guaranteed income in retirement.

14. Education and Skills: Investing in education, certifications, or acquiring new skills can increase earning potential and career opportunities.

15. Savings and Emergency Fund: Building a savings account and emergency fund provides liquidity and financial security during unexpected expenses or economic downturns.

Diversifying investments across various asset classes can help mitigate risk and maximize returns, ultimately leading to financial freedom and long-term wealth accumulation.

Common liabilities that can hinder individuals from achieving financial freedom.

1. Debt: High-interest consumer debt, such as credit card debt, personal loans, or payday loans, can drain financial resources and limit the ability to save and invest.

2. Mortgage: While a mortgage can be considered a liability, it's important to manage it effectively to avoid being burdened by excessive debt and high monthly payments.

3. Car Loans: Financing a vehicle purchase through a loan can result in monthly payments and interest costs, reducing cash flow available for savings and investments.

4. Student Loans: Education loans can saddle individuals with significant debt, impacting their ability to save for retirement or achieve other financial goals.

5. Medical Bills: Unexpected healthcare expenses or medical debt can strain finances and lead to financial stress if not properly managed.

6. Taxes: High tax liabilities or unpaid taxes can eat into disposable income and reduce the amount available for saving and investing.

7. Legal Obligations: Legal judgments, settlements, or lawsuits can result in financial obligations that deplete assets and hinder financial progress.

8. Family Support: Providing financial support to family members, such as aging parents or unemployed relatives, can strain resources and delay financial independence.

9. Overspending: Living beyond one's means and excessive spending on non-essential items can lead to debt accumulation and hinder wealth-building efforts.

10. Poor Financial Habits: Lack of budgeting, impulse buying, and failure to save regularly can impede progress toward financial freedom.

11. Lack of Insurance: Insufficient or inadequate insurance coverage for health, disability, life, or property can leave individuals vulnerable to financial setbacks in the event of emergencies or accidents.

12. Bad Investments: Poor investment decisions or speculative ventures can result in financial losses and setbacks on the path to financial freedom.

13. Lifestyle Inflation: Increasing spending habits to match rising income levels can prevent individuals from saving and investing enough to achieve financial independence.

14. Economic Downturns: Job loss, recession, or economic downturns can disrupt income streams and derail financial plans, making it challenging to achieve financial freedom.

15. Procrastination: Delaying financial planning, saving, or investing can prolong the journey to financial freedom and limit wealth accumulation over time.

Addressing and mitigating these liabilities through prudent financial management, debt reduction strategies, and disciplined saving and investing can help individuals overcome obstacles and progress toward financial independence.

Cash Flow

Cash flow refers to the movement of money in and out of a business or individual's finances over a specific period. It represents the inflow and outflow of cash resulting from various activities, such as operating, investing, and financing.

There are three main types of cash flow:

1. Operating Cash Flow (OCF): This type of cash flow reflects the cash generated or used in the daily operations of a business. It includes revenue from sales, payments to suppliers, wages, and other operational expenses.

2. Investing Cash Flow (ICF): Investing cash flow accounts for the purchase and sale of long-term assets, such as property, equipment, and investments. Positive investing cash flow indicates that a business or individual is investing in assets, while negative cash flow suggests divestment or selling of assets.

3. Financing Cash Flow (FCF): Financing cash flow tracks the cash flows related to raising capital and repaying debt. It includes proceeds from borrowing, repayments of loans, issuance or repurchase of stocks, and payment of dividends.

Positive cash flow occurs when the cash inflows exceed the outflows, indicating that more money is coming in than going out. This surplus cash can be used to fund operations, invest in growth opportunities, pay off debts, or distribute to shareholders. Conversely, negative cash flow occurs when the cash outflows exceed the inflows, indicating that more money is going out than coming in. While negative cash flow may be sustainable in the short term, it can lead to financial difficulties if not addressed promptly, as it may require borrowing or liquidating assets to cover expenses.

Cash flow analysis is essential for businesses and individuals to understand their financial health, manage liquidity, and make informed decisions about budgeting, investment, and financing activities. It provides insights into the ability to meet financial obligations, generate profits, and sustain long-term growth.

Create Positive Cash Flow

Positive cash flow is a financial term used to describe the situation where the cash inflows generated by an individual or entity exceed the cash outflows. In simpler terms, it means that you are earning more money than you are spending. Positive cash flow is a crucial component of financial stability and can have significant benefits for your financial freedom:

1. Debt Reduction: With positive cash flow, you have the ability to allocate more funds towards paying off debt, whether it's credit card balances, student loans, or mortgage payments. By reducing debt, you free up more of your income for savings and investments, ultimately accelerating your journey towards financial independence.

2. Savings and Investments: Positive cash flow provides you with the opportunity to save and invest for the future. Whether you're building an emergency fund, saving for retirement, or investing in assets such as stocks, real estate, or business ventures, having surplus cash allows you to grow your wealth over time and achieve your financial goals.

3. Financial Security: Maintaining positive cash flow acts as a buffer against unexpected expenses or financial emergencies. Having extra cash on hand provides you with a safety net to cover unforeseen costs without resorting to borrowing or tapping into savings, thereby safeguarding your financial security and peace of mind.

4. Lifestyle Flexibility: Positive cash flow affords you the freedom to make choices about how you want to live your life. Whether it's pursuing your passions, traveling, or indulging in hobbies and interests, having financial breathing room allows you to enjoy life without being constrained by financial constraints.

5. Wealth Accumulation: Over time, consistently positive cash flow enables you to accumulate wealth and build a solid financial foundation. By consistently reinvesting your surplus income into income-generating assets or high-yield investments, you can harness the power of compounding and exponentially grow your wealth over time, ultimately achieving financial freedom and independence.

In essence, positive cash flow is the lifeblood of financial freedom, providing you with the means to reduce debt, build savings, invest for the future, and enjoy a more secure and fulfilling life. By managing your cash flow effectively and prioritizing smart financial decisions, you can harness the power of positive cash flow to achieve your long-term financial goals and aspirations.

Chapter 4: Overcoming Financial Obstacles

As Michael continued to settle in to his new role, he found himself facing a host of financial obstacles. Despite the challenges of adjusting to life in a war zone and learning new skills on the job, one of the most pressing memories of this journey for Michael was the living conditions in Plywood Palace. The stifling heat, the relentless mosquitoes, and the frequent dust storms made each day a struggle, leaving him feeling disheartened and weary during that time.

Yet, amidst the hardships, there was a glimmer of hope—a beacon of light in the darkness. Two weeks into his new position, Michael received his paycheck in full for the first time after leaving Kuwait. —a life-changing sum that exceeded his wildest expectations. As he stared at the numbers in his bank account, his mind raced with possibilities. It was a pivotal moment—a turning point in his journey towards financial freedom. Michael had received 4 times the amount of his previous job for 2 weeks of work. More than Michael had received working for 4 months at his old job. He now saw the possibilities he could achieve with this one check.

For Michael, the deposit represented more than just a paycheck— it was a symbol of his determination and resilience in the face of adversity. It was proof that his hard work and perseverance were finally paying off, paving the way for a brighter future for himself and his loved ones. And as he reflected on the journey that had brought him to this moment, he knew that it was time to take control of his financial destiny.

With the deposit serving as a catalyst for change, Michael's journey towards financial independence took a significant turn when he found mentors who provided invaluable guidance and insight. Among these mentors was Mr. Reid, a retired disabled military veteran with a wealth of knowledge and experience in personal finance. Despite facing his own challenges, Mr. Reid always took the time to help Michael understand the principles of financial independence and wealth-building. Mr. Reid was only passing through to return to his own site but this small interaction with him started if shift in how Michael started to think about his finances.

As Michael delved deeper into his quest for financial freedom, he turned to books for inspiration and education. One book that profoundly impacted him was "Rich Dad Poor Dad" by Robert Kiyosaki. This timeless classic offered a fresh perspective on money management and challenged traditional beliefs about wealth accumulation. Michael found himself captivated by Kiyosaki's teachings and eager to apply them to his own financial journey.

Michael wasted no time in taking action. He began to scrutinize his expenses, identifying areas where he could cut back and save money. He set ambitious financial goals for himself, determined to build a secure future for himself and his family. And most importantly, he embraced a mindset of abundance, recognizing that he had the power to create the life of his dreams through hard work and determination.

Through his conversations with Mr. Reid and his exploration of financial literature, Michael began to gain a clearer understanding of the steps needed to achieve financial independence. He realized that building wealth required more than just hard work—it required strategic planning, discipline, and a willingness to challenge conventional wisdom.

Inspired by his newfound knowledge, Michael started to compile a list of "To Dos" aimed at accelerating his journey towards financial freedom. These included:

1. **Investing in Education**: Recognizing the importance of continuous learning, Michael made a commitment to invest in his education. Whether through books, courses, or seminars, he sought out opportunities to expand his knowledge and skills in areas such as personal finance, investing, and entrepreneurship.

2. **Setting Clear Financial Goals:** Michael understood the importance of setting clear, actionable goals to guide his financial journey. He identified specific milestones he wanted to achieve, such as paying off debt, building an emergency fund, and investing for the future.

3. Creating a Budget: Armed with insights from "Rich Dad Poor Dad" and advice from Mr. Reid, Michael created a detailed budget to track his income and expenses. This allowed him to identify areas where he could cut back on spending and redirect funds towards his debt and financial goals.

4. Building Multiple Streams of Income: Michael recognized the importance of diversifying his income sources to achieve financial security. In addition to his primary job, he explored opportunities for side jobs, and passive income streams such as real estate and investments.

5. Protecting Assets: Understanding the importance of asset protection, Michael took steps to safeguard his current assets against potential risks and liabilities. This included obtaining adequate insurance coverage and exploring ways to protect his one main asset, his home.

6. Networking and Seeking Guidance: Michael understood the value of surrounding himself with like-minded individuals who shared his passion for financial independence. He actively sought out mentors, created networking groups, and attended local gatherings to expand his circle of influence and gain valuable insights from others.

7. Staying Disciplined and Persistent: Above all, Michael remained disciplined and persistent in pursuit of his financial goals. He understood that achieving financial independence would require dedication, patience, and unwavering commitment to his long-term vision.

By incorporating these "To Dos" into his daily life, Michael began to see tangible progress towards his goal of financial independence within the first few months. With each step forward, he grew more confident in his ability to take control of his financial future and create the life of his dreams. And with mentors like Mr. Reid by he could call upon, guiding him every step of the way, Michael knew that nothing could stand in the way of his success. Michael faced significant financial challenges, including credit card debt, a second mortgage, first mortgage, student loans and vehicle debt, which threatened to hinder his path to financial freedom.

Recognizing the need for a strategic approach, and on top of his to-do list, Michael took the first step by creating a comprehensive plan.

This plan served as a roadmap, outlining his debts, and setting clear goals for repayment. Despite always paying his bills on time, Michael realized that making only the minimum payments was prolonging his debt. However, with a solid plan in place, he felt empowered to take control of his financial future.

So, the next things Michael did was:

I. Create a Detailed Budget: Start by tracking your income and expenses to understand where your money is going each month. Allocate a portion of your income towards debt repayment while ensuring you cover essential expenses.

2. List Your Debts: Make a list of all your debts, including balances, interest rates, and minimum monthly payments. This will help you prioritize which debts to pay off first.

3. Use the Smallest First Method: Begin by paying off the smallest debt first while continuing to make minimum payments on all other debts. Once the smallest debt is paid off, roll the payment amount into the next smallest debt, and so on. Another option is to pay off the highest interest debt first so you can save money on interest payments each month.

4. Cut Back on Expenses: Identify areas where you can cut back on non-essential expenses to free up more money for debt repayment. This could include dining out less, canceling subscription services, or finding more affordable alternatives.

5. Increase Your Income: Look for opportunities to increase your income, such as taking on a side hustle or freelancing gigs. Every extra dollar earned can be put towards paying off debt faster.

6. Negotiate with Creditors: Reach out to your creditors to negotiate lower interest rates or more favorable repayment terms. Many creditors are willing to work with borrowers facing financial difficulties to help them repay their debts.

7. Build an Emergency Fund: While focusing on debt repayment, it's important to have a safety net in place for unexpected expenses. Aim to build an emergency fund of at least three to six months' worth of living expenses to avoid relying on credit cards for emergencies.

8. Stay Motivated: Set small, achievable goals along the way to keep yourself motivated. Celebrate each debt paid off as a milestone towards financial freedom.

9. Avoid Taking on New Debt: Resist the temptation to take on new debt while you're working towards paying off existing debts. Avoid using credit cards for non-essential purchases and stick to your budget. Try to use cash to pay for items and if you can't afford it, think twice, and DO NOT proceed to make the purchase.

10. Seek Support: Don't hesitate to reach out for support from friends, family, or financial advisors. Having someone to hold you accountable and provide encouragement can make a big difference in staying on track with your debt repayment goals.

Obstacles

One of the first obstacles Michael tackled was his credit card debt. He identified more than seven credit cards with varying balances and interest rates, and he made it his priority to pay them off. By allocating additional funds to each card, starting with the smallest balance, and working his way up, Michael was able to eliminate this high-interest debt within a reasonable timeframe.

Next on Michael's list was his vehicle loan. By increasing his monthly payments and making extra contributions whenever possible, he accelerated the payoff process and reduced the overall interest costs. This proactive approach allowed him to free up more funds for tackling his remaining debts.

One of the most daunting challenges for Michael was his multiple student loan debts. With multiple balances and long-term repayment schedule, it seemed like a daunting mountain to climb. However, Michael remained determined and focused on his goal of becoming debt-free. He explored options for refinancing to lower interest rates and devised a plan to increase his monthly payments, chipping away at the debt little by little. Michael then thought, refinancing wasn't an option because refinancing would take more money away. Michael stayed focused on the task at hand and continued to chip away at the debt as it was.

As Michael continued to make progress on his debt repayment journey, he also addressed his second mortgage. By applying the same strategies of increased payments, he was able to expedite the payoff process and save money on interest in the long run. Each milestone achieved brought him one step closer to financial freedom. Michael also recognized the value of seeking support and advice from financial experts and mentors. Their guidance helped him navigate the complexities of debt repayment and stay motivated during challenging times.

Surrounding himself with a supportive network of friends far from home provided encouragement and accountability along the way. As the weeks turned into months, Michael's financial situation continued to improve. With each paycheck, he grew closer to achieving his goals, building a solid foundation for a future filled with prosperity and abundance. And as he looked back on his journey, he knew that overcoming financial obstacles was just the beginning it was the first step on the path to a life of limitless possibilities.

After some months of intensive training and preparation in BIAP, Michael felt ready to tackle the challenges awaiting him in at his newly assigned location in TAJI Iraq. Armed with a wealth of knowledge and newfound confidence, he was eager to put his training to the test as he embarked on the next phase of his journey. It was time to leave behind the confines of the Plywood Palace and venture out into the field, where he would manage four other locations across Iraq.

As Michael settled into his new base and assumed his responsibilities, he reunited with a figure who had already profoundly impacted his journey Mr. Reid, affectionately known as Unc. Mr. Reid was more than just a mentor; he was the company site lead and a guiding light amidst the chaos of war-torn Iraq. With his wealth of experience and sage advice, he quickly became a trusted confidant and source of inspiration for Michael.

Under Mr. Reid's tutelage, Michael began to navigate the intricacies of managing multiple locations in a volatile environment. He learned valuable lessons about leadership, decision-making, and adaptability skills that would serve him well in the years to come. But perhaps most importantly, he learned the true meaning of resilience and determination in the face of adversity. In the initial stages of Michael's journey in his new location, he embarked on a series of exhilarating experiences that reshaped his perspective on change. Among these adventures was the opportunity to travel from site to site aboard Black Hawk and Chinook helicopters, which served as the primary mode of transportation across the expansive landscape of Iraq. For

Michael, these airborne journeys were not just a means of getting from point A to point B; they represented a thrilling departure from the familiar and a gateway to new horizons. The sensation of soaring through the skies, with the wind rushing past and the ground far below, instilled in him a sense of awe and wonder that transcended the challenges of his surroundings. In those moments suspended between earth and sky, Michael found a newfound appreciation for the transformative power of change, embracing each flight as a symbol of his willingness to venture beyond the confines of his comfort zone and embrace the unknown.

Amidst the exhilarating experiences of traversing Iraq, Michael found himself immersed in a world of camaraderie and collaboration. As he traveled to various sites, he had the privilege of meeting the site leads of each site, who welcomed him with open arms. Their warm reception was not merely a gesture of hospitality; it was a testament to the common purpose that united them – the shared mission of improving operational efficiency and ensuring the success of their endeavors in challenging environments. Quickly integrating into the fabric of these teams, Michael forged bonds of friendship and mentorship with the site leads, many of whom were retired military personnel themselves. Their wealth of experience and knowledge, both war zones and of financial freedom, proved invaluable to Michael as he navigated the complexities of his surroundings. In their guidance and mentorship, he found not only invaluable insights but also a sense of camaraderie and belonging that fortified his resolve to overcome any obstacle in pursuit of his goals.

As Michael forged ahead in his new role, he encountered countless challenges and obstacles along the way. From navigating bureaucratic red tape to dealing with security threats and logistical nightmares, there was never a dull moment in Iraq. Yet, with Mr. Reid by his side, he faced each challenge head-on, drawing strength from their shared experiences and unwavering resolve.

Together, Michael and Mr. Reid weathered the storms of uncertainty and upheaval, emerging stronger and more resilient with each passing day. Their bond transcended the boundaries of mentorship, evolving into a lifelong friendship built on trust, mutual respect, and shared aspirations. And as they worked tirelessly to overcome the obstacles that stood in their way, they forged a path towards success that would inspire generations to come.

But their journey was far from over. As Michael delved deeper into his role and assumed greater responsibilities, he encountered new opportunities and challenges that would push him to his limits. Yet, through it all, he remained steadfast in his commitment to excellence, determined to make the most of every opportunity that came his way.

As the days turned into weeks and the weeks into months, Michael's journey continued to unfold, revealing new layers of complexity and depth with each passing day. And as he reflected on the path that had led him to this moment, he couldn't help but marvel at the remarkable twists and turns of fate that had brought him here. For in the midst of uncertainty and chaos, he had found purpose, meaning, and a sense of fulfillment that transcended the challenges of the present moment.

Working with Mr. Reid, Michael embarked on a journey of self-discovery and transformation—a journey that would ultimately lead him to the keys of financial success and the fulfillment of his deepest dreams. And as he looked towards the horizon, he knew that the best was yet to come.

As Michael followed his mentor and list of To-do's for the first 6 months, Michael diligently worked towards paying off his credit cards and worked on his student loan debts over the course of six months, he celebrated each milestone achieved along the journey. Whether it was paying off a credit card or making a significant dent in his student loan balance, these victories served as fuel for his motivation to keep pushing forward.

With each debt eliminated, he felt a sense of liberation and empowerment, knowing that he was taking control of his financial future. He looked forward to planning a special trip home for Christmas. It had been six months since he had last seen his family, and the thought of reuniting with them filled him with joy and anticipation. Even as Michael's mindset about finances shifted towards that of a millionaire's, he harbored a desire to indulge his family, a gesture that had been rare in his upbringing. Determined to make this Christmas unforgettable, Michael resolved to spoil his loved ones in ways they had never experienced before.

Upon arriving home, Michael wasted no time in making preparations for the holiday season. He had asked his son Zyon, nephew Malik, mother, father, and sister what they wanted for Christmas weeks before arriving home. Michael had promised to himself he would fulfill their wishes no matter the cost. With his generous income from his job in Iraq, Michael was determined to spoil his family and show them how much they meant to him.

The Christmas that followed was nothing short of magical. Family and friends gathered from far and wide to celebrate the joyous occasion, turning the family home into a bustling hub of laughter and love. It was a true family reunion, filled with warmth, nostalgia, and the spirit of togetherness.

Little did Michael know at this time; this would be the last Christmas and the last days he would spend with his father. Before Michael left to return in Iraq, his father fell ill but his words to Michael was "I'll be alright son, go back and continue your journey" Michael was a bit relieved and had vowed to stay beside his father but his father insisted to not miss his flight back to Iraq. Michael's father eventually went home soon after Michael left, and Michael was happy to hear that all things were now going well.

Tragically, after Michael returned to Iraq in January, in the heart of Iraq, amidst the chaos of war and uncertainty, Michael's world came crashing down with the late-night constant on January 20th inauguration day, a piercing ring of his phone repeatedly. He fumbled to answer, his fingers trembling with anticipation, but the crackling static on the line only added to his frustration. Michael didn't recognize the number, but he knew the area code was from his home city. Desperate to hear the voice on the other end, he strained his ears against the interference, but the words remained elusive. Michael had never received so many phone calls from home, especially late in the midnight hours. The signal was bad, and Michael couldn't hear a thing.

With a sinking feeling in his chest, Michael made a snap decision. He knew something had to be wrong to keep receiving the same phone call repeatedly. Ignoring the persistent calls for his attention, he hastily made his way to the relative quiet of his office where he knew he could contact the number with ease, the urgency of the situation urging him forward. Each minute felt heavier than the last, his heart pounding in his ears as he prayed for a glimmer of hope amidst the turmoil. Once inside his office, Michael wasted no time dialing the unknown number, his hands trembling as he held the receiver to his ear. With bated breath, he waited for someone to pick up on the other end, his pulse racing with anticipation.

Finally, a voice broke through the silence, and Michael's heart skipped a beat. It was his cousin Christopher, his usually jovial tone strained with emotion. And then, the words that shattered Michael's world into a million pieces.

"He's gone, Michael. He's gone."

Time seemed to stand still as Michael processed the devastating news, his mind reeling with disbelief. Michael could not understand what was said and was in denial and major disbelief. Michael replied WHO? Who's gone? It wasn't until Michael's sister Valerie took command of the phone and again said these words in a crying, trembling, and shaking voice.

"Michael, father is dead, he's dead"

In an instant, the world around him faded into insignificance as he collapsed to his knees, the weight of his grief crushing him like a tidal wave. Tears streamed down his face unchecked, his cries of anguish echoing off the walls of his silent office as he grappled with the enormity of his loss. In that moment of profound despair, Michael felt as though the ground had been ripped out from beneath him, leaving him adrift in a sea of sorrow. Michael's father had died from a blood clot.

As the reality of his father's passing sank in, Michael clung to the memories they had shared, each one a precious treasure to be cherished for eternity. Though the pain of his loss would never truly fade, he found solace in the love and support of those around him, drawing strength from their unwavering presence in his darkest hour.

And as he knelt there in the silence of his office, surrounded by the echoes of his grief, Michael had to bring himself together and plan a way to immediately get out of Iraq and back home to his family. Michael was deeply saddened in Iraq. It took 2 days for Michael to make his way out of the war-torn country. During the 16-hour flight home, Michael sat and wrote his father's obituary and vowed to honor his father's memory by carrying on his legacy with courage and grace. For though his father may be gone, his spirit would live on in the hearts of those who loved him, forever guiding them through the trials and tribulations of life.

In the wake of his father's passing, Michael found himself thrust into a new role – that of the leader of the family. His father had been a pillar of strength and guidance, and now Michael was tasked with filling his shoes. It was a daunting challenge, akin to facing Goliath, but Michael knew he had to step up for the sake of his family.

Despite the immense grief weighing heavily on his heart, Michael remained resolute in his determination to honor his father's legacy. He drew strength from the lessons his father had imparted over the years, channeling his wisdom and courage as he navigated the challenges of leading his family through their time of mourning.

In the midst of his grief, Michael found solace in the love and support of his family and friends. Together, they leaned on each other for strength, finding comfort in their shared memories and the bond that held them together. As the days turned into weeks and the weeks into months, Michael slowly began to come to terms with his father's passing. While the pain of loss would always linger, he found peace in knowing that his father's spirit lived on in the love and memories they shared.

As Michael sat alone in the quiet of his room the weight of his father's passing always hung heavy on his shoulders. For Michael, it felt as if his father was still back home living a normal life because he was not there to experience the days without his father being around. During his grief, a sudden realization dawned on him, like a beacon of light piercing through the darkness of his sorrow. With his heart heavy and his mind racing, Michael began to see his circumstances in a new light. Perhaps, he thought, there was a reason he had been placed in this position in Iraq, far from home and family. Maybe, just maybe, it was all part of a greater plan—a plan orchestrated by a higher power.

As this realization washed over him, Michael's eyes widened in awe and understanding. Could it be that God had placed him in this position for a purpose greater than he had ever imagined? Was he meant to be here, in this war-torn land, to provide for his family in their time of need? The thought filled Michael with a sense of purpose and clarity unlike anything he had ever experienced before. Suddenly, the sacrifices he had made and the challenges he had faced seemed to pale in comparison to the profound sense of duty that now coursed through his veins.

And so, as he sat there in the silence of his room, surrounded by the echoes of his grief, Michael made a silent vow to himself and to his father's memory. He would carry on his legacy with courage and strength, knowing that he had been chosen for a purpose far greater than he could ever have imagined. His Families Chosen One!

Michael found himself thrust into a new role as the pillar of strength for his family. As the chosen leader, he understood the weight of responsibility resting on his shoulders and knew that he needed to buckle down and face the challenges ahead with unwavering determination. With a renewed sense of purpose, Michael made it his mission to overcome the obstacle of debt that lingered over his family and to chart a course towards a brighter financial future for both him and his loved ones.

Michael vowed to embrace his role as the provider for his family, leading his family with compassion, strength, and unwavering love to honor his father's memory by stepping into the shoes he had left behind. Though the road ahead would undoubtedly be fraught with difficulty and uncertainty, Michael knew that he was not alone. He had been called to this task for a reason, and with faith as his guide, he would rise to meet the challenges ahead and as he faced the challenges that lay ahead, he carried his father's spirit with him, guiding him every step of the way.

The passing of Michael's father marked a profound turning point in his life, one that presented both emotional turmoil and renewed determination. Amidst the grief and loss, Michael found within himself a newfound sense of purpose, a resolve to honor his father's memory by taking charge of his financial future. With a steely determination born of adversity, Michael embarked on a journey to unlock the millionaire within and overcome the obstacles that stood between him and financial freedom.

In the wake of his father's death, Michael confronted his debts with a newfound sense of urgency, recognizing that his financial obligations were not merely burdens but opportunities for growth and transformation. Armed with this perspective, he adopted an initiative-taking approach to debt management, devising strategies to reduce his liabilities and streamline his finances. With disciplined budgeting and strategic planning, Michael gradually chipped away at his debts, one payment at a time, inching closer to his goal of financial independence.

Moreover, Michael's father's passing served as a poignant reminder of the fragility of life and the importance of making the most of every opportunity. Fueled by this realization, Michael embraced a mindset of abundance and possibility, seeking out new avenues for income generation and wealth accumulation. From exploring new investment opportunities to leveraging his skills and expertise in the workplace, Michael seized every chance to expand his financial horizons and secure a brighter future for himself and his loved ones.

In overcoming the adversity of his father's death, Michael emerged not only stronger but also more resilient and resourceful. His journey toward financial freedom became not just a means to an end but a testament to the indomitable human spirit and the power of perseverance in the face of adversity. With each obstacle he conquered and each milestone he achieved, Michael moved closer to realizing his dreams and creating a legacy that would endure long after him.

Overcoming

In the journey towards financial freedom and prosperity, one of the most crucial steps is understanding how to effectively manage and pay off debt. Debt can weigh heavily on individuals, stifling their ability to build wealth and achieve their financial goals. However, by embracing change and adopting a strategic approach to debt repayment, individuals can take control of their finances and pave the way towards a brighter future.

One key principle to keep in mind when tackling debt is the concept of prioritizing payments based on interest rates. The higher the interest rate on a debt, the more it costs you each month in interest charges. Therefore, it makes financial sense to prioritize paying off debts with the highest interest rates first, as this will ultimately save you money in the long run.

By focusing on paying off high-interest debts first, individuals can minimize the amount of money they lose each month to interest charges. This frees up more funds to put towards other financial goals, such as building an emergency fund, investing for the future, or saving for major purchases. Additionally, prioritizing high-interest debt repayment can help individuals break free from the cycle of debt more quickly. By eliminating debts with the highest interest rates first, individuals can reduce the total amount of interest they pay over time, allowing them to pay off their debts faster and save money in the process.

Another benefit of prioritizing high-interest debt repayment is the psychological impact it can have. As individuals see their debts decrease and their financial situation improve, they may feel more motivated and empowered to continue making progress towards their financial goals.

To effectively prioritize debt repayment, it's important for individuals to take stock of their current financial situation and make a plan. This may involve creating a budget, identifying all outstanding debts, and determining the interest rates associated with each debt.

Once individuals have a clear understanding of their debts and interest rates, they can develop a repayment strategy that focuses on paying off high-interest debts first while making minimum payments on lower-interest debts. This may involve allocating extra funds towards high-interest debts each month or using strategies such as the debt snowball or debt avalanche method to accelerate repayment taught by Mr. Dave Ramsey.

Ultimately, by embracing change and prioritizing high-interest debt repayment, individuals can take control of their finances, reduce their debt burden, and pave the way towards a brighter financial future. With determination, discipline, and a strategic approach, anyone can achieve financial freedom and build wealth for the long term.

Chapter 5: The Power of Saving and Budgeting

In the pursuit of financial stability and wealth accumulation, few practices are as fundamental as budgeting and saving. These two pillars form the cornerstone of sound financial management, laying the groundwork for long-term success and prosperity.

In this chapter, we will explore the significance of budgeting and saving, as well as strategies for setting and achieving savings goals amidst various financial obligations. Michael's journey towards financial stability in Iraq was marked by unwavering determination and laser focus. Despite the challenges of living and working in a war zone, he recognized the importance of budgeting and saving as foundational steps towards achieving his long-term financial goals. With a clear vision in mind, Michael set out to save $50,000 for a rainy day while simultaneously tackling his debt. This is not the typical approach because Michael wasn't fully aware of the best steps for saving.

It wasn't an easy task. With a long deployment ahead of him, Michael knew he had to be disciplined and strategic in his approach. He started by meticulously tracking his expenses and identifying areas where he could cut back. Every dollar saved was a step closer to his goal, and Michael was determined to make the most of his limited resources.

As we mentioned in previous chapters, the first hurdle Michael faced was paying off his credit card debt. With high interest rates eating away at his income, he knew he had to tackle this obstacle head-on. Through careful budgeting and sacrifice, Michael managed to eliminate his credit card debt within the first 3-4 months of his deployment. It was a significant milestone and a testament to his commitment to financial freedom.

Next on the list were his student loans and car payment. Again, Michael approached these debts with laser focus, allocating extra funds each month towards their repayment. Redirecting all the credit card payment money to the new bills. This was now known as the debt snowball by "David Ramsey" but Michael didn't know anything about

Dave Ramsey at the time. In later Chapters through reading and learning Michael found that Dave Ramsey's methods were true because he was witnessing it first hand. It wasn't easy paying off these debts while wanting to enjoy the money and his new life, but with perseverance and determination, he was able to pay off both debts the student loans and car within the span of a year.

Despite making significant progress, Michael still had his second mortgage and first mortgage on his house looming over him. While these debts would take longer to pay off, he remained undeterred. With each passing month, he chipped away at his mortgage balances, inching closer to financial freedom.

Throughout his journey, Michael leaned on the support and guidance of his colleagues and mentor. Constant talks with them helped him stay on track and remain focused on his goals. Their encouragement and advice served as a constant source of motivation, reminding Michael of the importance of staying disciplined and committed to his financial objectives.

In addition to paying off debt, Michael also prioritized saving for emergencies and future expenses. By setting aside a portion of his income each month, he gradually built up a rainy day fund of $50,000. This financial cushion provided him with peace of mind and security, knowing that he was prepared for whatever challenges lay ahead.

Michael's experience underscores the significance of budgeting and saving as foundational steps towards financial stability and wealth accumulation. By taking control of his finances and making strategic decisions, he was able to achieve his goals and pave the way for a brighter future. His story serves as inspiration for others embarking on their own journey towards financial freedom, demonstrating that with determination and discipline, anything is possible.

Budgeting serves as a roadmap for managing expenses and income, providing clarity and control over one's financial situation. By creating a budget, individuals gain insight into their spending habits and can identify areas where adjustments may be needed to align with their financial goals. Moreover, budgeting enables individuals to prioritize savings, ensuring that a portion of their income is set aside for future needs and goals.

Saving, on the other hand, is the act of setting aside a portion of income for future use or emergencies. It serves as a buffer against unexpected expenses and provides financial security and peace of mind. Whether saving for a down payment on a home, an emergency fund, or retirement, the habit of saving regularly is essential for building wealth over time.

When it comes to setting and achieving savings goals while budgeting for various expenses, it's essential to adopt a strategic approach tailored to individual circumstances. Here are some strategies for managing savings goals amidst common financial obligations:

Fixed Costs-50%-60% of your gross monthly income:

1. Housing Expenses: Allocate a portion of your budget towards housing expenses, including rent or mortgage payments, property taxes, insurance, and maintenance costs. Consider exploring cost-saving measures such as downsizing or refinancing to free up funds for savings.

2. Credit Card Debt: Prioritize paying off high-interest credit card debt by allocating extra funds towards monthly payments. Consider consolidating debt or negotiating lower interest rates to accelerate repayment and redirect savings towards other financial goals.

3. Personal Loans: Include monthly payments for personal loans in your budget and explore opportunities to accelerate repayment, such as making bi-weekly payments or paying more than the minimum amount due.

4. Student Loans: Develop a repayment plan for student loans based on your financial situation and prioritize paying off loans with the highest interest rates first. Explore options for loan consolidation or refinancing to lower monthly payments and free up funds for savings.

5. Car Loans: Factor monthly car loan payments into your budget and consider refinancing or selling the vehicle if payments are unmanageable. Redirect savings from lower interest rates or reduced loan balances towards other financial goals.

6. Business Loans: If you have business loans, incorporate monthly payments into your budget and explore opportunities to increase revenue or reduce expenses to free up funds for savings.

7. Second Mortgages: Include monthly payments for second mortgages in your budget and consider refinancing or restructuring the loan to lower interest rates and reduce monthly payments.

8. Additional Debt: Take stock of any additional debts, such as medical bills or personal lines of credit, and incorporate monthly payments into your budget. Prioritize repayment based on interest rates and explore options for reducing or eliminating debt to accelerate savings.

Michael's story is a testament to the importance of managing finances and striving towards financial freedom. In his journey to become debt-free, Michael tackled various debts, including credit card debt, student loans, car payments, and mortgages. These debts are what we call fixed costs—they typically remain consistent until they are fully paid off.

To manage these fixed costs effectively, it's crucial to allocate a portion of your income towards debt repayment. Experts suggest dedicating between 50% to 60% of your gross monthly income to fixed debts. This ensures that you are making steady progress towards paying off your debts without overwhelming your financial plan. However, it's essential not to exceed the 60% threshold, as this can negatively impact other areas of your financial goals and plans.

By adhering to this principle, individuals can establish a structured approach to debt repayment while maintaining financial stability. Allocating a significant portion of your income towards fixed debts allows you to make consistent payments and gradually reduce your outstanding balances over time. This disciplined approach lays the foundation for achieving financial freedom and building wealth in the long run.

Moreover, by prioritizing debt repayment and staying within the recommended allocation range, individuals can avoid excessive financial strain and mitigate the risk of falling into further debt. It provides a sense of control and empowerment, knowing that you are actively working towards improving your financial situation and securing your future.

Ultimately, Michael's journey serves as a reminder of the importance of budgeting and saving, particularly when it comes to managing fixed debts. By adopting a strategic approach and adhering to established guidelines, individuals can take control of their finances, become debt-free, and pave the way towards a brighter financial future.

Savings: 10% of your gross Monthly Income:

Michael's journey towards saving 10% of his income and ultimately accumulating $50,000 was not without its challenges and mindset shifts. Initially, Michael didn't start with the intention of saving a specific percentage of his income; rather, he set his sights on a specific financial milestone—$50,000. This ambitious goal represented a significant sum, one that Michael had never seen in his life. However, he was determined to pursue it, recognizing the transformative potential it held for his financial future.

At first, the idea of saving $50,000 seemed daunting to Michael. It required discipline, sacrifice, and a fundamental shift in mindset. Yet, he understood that achieving this goal would propel him towards greater financial freedom and open doors to opportunities he had only dreamed of. With this target in mind, Michael approached saving with renewed determination and focus.

To kickstart his savings journey, Michael began by setting aside a fixed percentage of his income each month. While it wasn't initially 10%, he adjusted his savings rate over time to align with his goal of accumulating $50,000. Every dollar saved brought him one step closer to his objective, fueling his motivation and resolve.

As Michael diligently saved and chipped away at his debts, he began to see progress towards his $50,000 goal. With each passing month, his savings grew, inching closer to the coveted milestone. It wasn't easy, and there were moments of doubt and uncertainty along the way. Yet, Michael remained steadfast in his commitment to achieving financial success.

With his debts nearing pay offs and close to $50,000 in savings achieved in his second year in Iraq, Michael found himself at a crossroad. He began to see what he was about to accomplish. What once seemed impossible, but he knew that his journey was far from over. Inspired by his success, Michael set his sights on an even loftier goal—the 100k club. If he could save $50,000, he reasoned, then reaching $100,000 was within his grasp.

Michael's journey serves as a powerful reminder of the transformative power of setting ambitious financial goals. By daring to dream big and taking proactive steps towards achieving his

objectives, he was able to defy expectations and chart a course towards greater financial security and abundance. Aspiring to save 10% of his income was just the beginning; with perseverance and determination, Michael proved that anything is possible.

Here's how to Budget and Save in your pursuit of financial freedom

Budgeting and saving a portion of your income—specifically 10% of your gross monthly income—play pivotal roles in achieving financial freedom and security. By adhering to this principle, you can build a solid financial foundation and safeguard yourself against unforeseen emergencies. Setting up automatic savings transfers to a separate account streamlines the process, ensuring consistent contributions without the need for manual intervention.

3-6 months expenses in emergency fund

You need to become a Master of your budget. Your budget is your guideline. It's your key to managing your income. It's your holy grail for financial freedom. Building an emergency fund, is a crucial component of financial stability and preparedness. One key principle emphasized is the need to save an adequate amount to cover 3-6 months' worth of expenses.

Why 3-6 months? This range is recommended to provide a buffer against unexpected financial setbacks, such as job loss, medical emergencies, or major home repairs. Having enough funds to cover several months of expenses ensures that you can weather financial storms without resorting to high-interest debt or depleting your savings.

To calculate your emergency fund target, start by tallying up your essential monthly expenses, including housing costs, utilities, groceries, transportation, insurance premiums, and debt payments. Multiply this total by the number of months you aim to save for (ideally between 3 and 6 months) to determine your target savings goal.

For example, if your monthly expenses amount to $3,000 and you aim to save for 6 months' worth of expenses, your target emergency fund would be $18,000 ($3,000 x 6).

Building this emergency fund requires discipline and commitment. If your're unable to save 10% of your income, start by setting aside a portion of your income each month specifically designated for your emergency fund. Consider automating transfers to a separate high yield savings account to ensure consistency and prevent temptation to spend.

As you contribute to your emergency fund over time, track your progress regularly and adjust your savings strategy as needed. Remember that emergencies can arise unexpectedly, so having this financial cushion in place provides peace of mind and greater financial resilience.

In conclusion, prioritizing the accumulation of 3-6 months worth of expenses in an emergency fund is a foundational step towards achieving financial stability and preparedness. By proactively saving for unforeseen circumstances, you can safeguard your financial well-being and mitigate the impact of unexpected events on your financial health.

Here are some steps to effectively save 10% of your gross monthly income

One game-changing option is to consider opening a high-yield savings account with reputable institutions such as SoFi, Wealthfront, or Ally, which currently offer competitive interest rates of up to 4.5%. Alternatively, leaving your savings in a traditional bank account may yield minimal returns, typically around 0.01%.

To maximize the potential of your savings, consider exploring a list of banks that offer higher interest rates to generate passive income. By strategically selecting an account with a higher interest rate, you can aim to earn a substantial monthly returns on your savings.

Ultimately, the key is to take proactive steps to grow your savings, leveraging high-yield savings accounts to maximize your earning potential and secure your financial future. By carefully selecting the right financial instruments and consistently saving a portion of your income, you can work towards building a solid foundation for long-term financial success.

Key Points

1. Assess Your Finances: Begin by evaluating your current financial situation. Calculate your gross monthly income and identify areas where you can trim expenses to allocate 10% towards savings.

2. Create a Budget: Develop a comprehensive budget that outlines your income and expenses. Allocate 10% of your gross monthly income towards savings as a non-negotiable expense, just like rent or utilities.

3. Set Up Automatic Transfers: Take advantage of your bank's automatic transfer feature to divert 10% of your income directly into a separate savings account or create a new high yield savings account as mentioned before to maximize your savings while your money sits. Automatic transfers remove the temptation to spend the money and ensures consistent savings contributions each month.

4. Reduce Discretionary Spending: Look for opportunities to cut back on non-essential expenses, such as dining out, entertainment, or subscription services. Redirect the funds saved towards your savings goal.

5. Increase Income: If necessary, consider seeking additional sources of income to supplement your primary earnings. This could involve taking on a part-time job, freelancing, or starting a side business. Allocate the extra income towards savings to accelerate your progress.

6. Prioritize Emergency Fund: Treat your savings as an emergency fund designed to provide financial support during times of need. Aim to build a cushion equivalent to at least three to six months' worth of living expenses to cover unexpected costs without resorting to loans or credit cards.

By adhering to these steps and consistently saving 10% of your gross monthly income, you can build a robust emergency fund that serves as a financial safety net. This fund not only provides peace of mind but also empowers you to navigate unexpected challenges without derailing your long-term financial goals. Start today, and take proactive steps towards achieving financial freedom and security.

Investing: 5%-10% of your gross Monthly Income

Michael's journey towards investing began with a realization sparked by conversations with colleagues, guidance from his mentor, and insights gained from various books on financial freedom. As he delved deeper into the world of personal finance, Michael discovered a common thread among these resources—investing. Recognizing the potential for wealth accumulation and financial growth through investing, he decided to allocate a portion of his income—5%-10%—towards general investing.

To kickstart his investment journey, Michael opted for online trading accounts such as TD Ameritrade, which offered user-friendly platforms and convenient access to a wide range of investment options. Setting up a free investment account was quick and easy, allowing him to begin investing with a small amount of capital.

Moreover, Michael recognized the importance of maximizing opportunities for investment offered by his employer's retirement plan. By enrolling in his company's 401(k) plan, Michael could take advantage of employer matching contributions, which matched 100% of his deposits up to 6% each year. This revelation was a wow moment for Michael, as he realized the potential to double his contributions with free money from his employer.

Initially, Michael viewed the employer match as a straightforward exchange—$100 in deposits equated to an additional $100 from the company. However, he soon discovered the compounding benefits of investing in his 401(k). Not only did his contributions earn dividends reinvested over time, but they also benefited from the average gain of 8%-10% in the stock market each year.

As Michael continued to invest and educate himself about various investment strategies and opportunities, he diversified his portfolio to include stocks, bonds, mutual funds, and other investment vehicles. He learned to balance risk and reward, aligning his investment choices with his long-term financial goals and risk tolerance.

Michael's journey into investing was a gradual progression that began once he had made significant strides in paying off his debts. In the initial stages of his debt payoff journey, investing was not on Michael's radar. His primary focus was on reducing his debt burden and achieving financial stability. It wasn't until approximately 80% of his debts were paid off that Michael began to explore the world of investing.

With a newfound sense of financial freedom and a desire to make his money work for him, Michael decided to dip his toes into the investment waters. Starting with a small amount of money, he sought to test the waters and gain firsthand experience in the world of investing.

Michael opted for a "lazy fund" approach to investing, which involved purchasing mutual funds and ETFs (exchange-traded funds). These investment vehicles offered him the opportunity to diversify his portfolio and gain exposure to a wide range of companies and industries with a single investment.

One of the key advantages of investing in mutual funds and ETFs, as Michael discovered, was the simplicity and convenience they offered. Rather than having to research and individually purchase multiple stocks, mutual funds and ETFs functioned like a shopping cart, allowing Michael to invest in a basket of stocks with ease.

Each mutual fund or ETF contained a diversified mix of stocks, bonds, or other assets, providing Michael with instant diversification and risk mitigation. This "set it and forget it" approach appealed to Michael, as it allowed him to passively invest in the market without the need for constant monitoring and management.

By embracing the lazy fund approach, Michael was able to overcome the intimidation and complexity often associated with investing. Instead of feeling overwhelmed by the prospect of selecting individual stocks, he could rely on the expertise of fund managers to make investment decisions on his behalf.

As Michael continued to gain confidence and experience in the world of investing, he diversified his portfolio further and explored other investment opportunities. However, the lazy fund approach served as a solid foundation for his investment journey, providing him with a simple yet effective strategy for building wealth over time.

Through disciplined investing and strategic decision-making, Michael steadily grew his investment portfolio, laying the groundwork for financial security and wealth accumulation. His journey serves as a testament to the transformative power of investing and highlights the importance of starting early and staying committed to one's financial goals. With each investment, Michael moved closer to realizing his vision of financial freedom and abundance.

Here are some steps to help you start your investment journey.

Starting to invest in mutual funds and ETFs can be a wise decision for building long-term wealth and financial security. Here are some steps to get started:

1. Pay Off High-Interest Debts: Before diving into investing, prioritize paying off any high-interest debts, such as credit card balances or personal loans. High-interest debt can eat away at your investment gains, making it essential to reduce this financial burden first.

2. Set Financial Goals: Define your financial goals and objectives. Determine your investment time horizon, risk tolerance, and desired outcomes. Whether you're saving for retirement, a down payment on a home, or your children's education, having clear goals will help guide your investment decisions.

3. Educate Yourself: Take the time to educate yourself about mutual funds and ETFs. Understand the differences between the two investment vehicles, their underlying assets, fees, and performance history. Consider reading books, articles, or taking online courses to expand your knowledge.

4. Assess Risk Tolerance: Assess your risk tolerance to determine the appropriate asset allocation for your investment portfolio. Consider factors such as your age, financial situation, and comfort level with market fluctuations. Mutual funds and ETFs offer a range of investment options tailored to different risk profiles.

5. Choose a Brokerage Account: Select a reputable brokerage platform that offers access to a wide range of mutual funds and ETFs. Look for low fees, user-friendly interfaces, and robust research tools. Popular brokerage platforms include Vanguard, Fidelity, Charles Schwab, and TD Ameritrade.

6. Research Funds: Conduct thorough research to identify mutual funds and ETFs that align with your investment objectives and risk tolerance. Consider factors such as fund performance, expense ratios, investment strategy, and historical returns. Look for funds with a history of consistent performance and low fees.

7. Diversify Your Portfolio: Diversification is key to managing risk and maximizing returns. Spread your investments across different asset classes, sectors, and geographic regions. Avoid putting all your money into a single fund or asset class to minimize the impact of market volatility. Mutual Funds and ETFs are the best way to diversify your portfolio.

8. Start Small: Begin investing with a small amount of money and gradually increase your contributions over time. This approach allows you to test the waters and gain experience without taking on excessive risk. Set up automatic contributions to your investment accounts to ensure consistent savings.

9. Monitor and Rebalance: Regularly review your investment portfolio and adjust as needed. Monitor fund performance, economic trends, and changes in your financial situation. Rebalance your portfolio periodically to maintain your desired asset allocation and risk profile. Mutual funds and ETFs don't need to be rebalanced often, but you could make adjustments in the overall fund you are investing in.

10. Stay Disciplined: Stay disciplined and avoid emotional decision-making during market fluctuations. Focus on your long-term investment objectives and resist the urge to react to short-term market volatility. Remember that investing is a marathon, not a sprint, and patience is key to success.

By following these steps and staying committed to your investment strategy, you can build a diversified portfolio of mutual funds and ETFs that aligns with your financial goals and helps you achieve long-term wealth accumulation.

Other Spending- Fun in the Sun: 20%-35% of your gross Monthly Income:

Michael understood the importance of balance in his financial journey, which is why he allocated a portion of his income—20%-35%—for what he fondly referred to as "fun in the sun." This allocation might seem substantial at first glance, but Michael recognized that it was essential for maintaining his overall well-being and happiness.

During the initial stages of paying off his debts, Michael prioritized financial discipline and restraint. He understood that every dollar saved and invested in debt repayment brought him one step closer to his ultimate goal of financial freedom. Consequently, he limited his discretionary spending and focused on achieving his debt repayment targets.

However, as Michael made progress in paying off his debts and building his savings, he began to incorporate the concept of "fun in the sun" into his budget. By aligning his expenses with the percentages previously allocated for housing, debt repayment, savings, investing and other necessities, Michael calculated an amount that he could comfortably allocate towards leisure activities and enjoyment.

This approach ensured that Michael could indulge in activities that brought him joy without compromising his long-term financial goals. Whether it was a weekend getaway, dining out with friends, or pursuing a hobby, Michael had the flexibility to enjoy life's pleasures while staying within his financial boundaries.

By adhering to this balanced approach, Michael found that he could maintain a healthy relationship with money. He avoided feelings of deprivation or guilt associated with excessive spending, knowing that he had accounted for fun in his budget responsibly.

Moreover, as Michael's financial situation improved and his debts were paid off, the percentage allocated for "fun in the sun" became more manageable. With fewer financial obligations weighing him down, he could allocate a larger portion of his income towards leisure activities while still prioritizing savings and investments for the future.

In essence, Michael's approach to budgeting and allocating percentages of his income allowed him to strike a harmonious balance between financial responsibility and enjoyment. By incorporating "fun in the sun" into his budgeting strategy, he could live a fulfilling and enjoyable life while staying on track towards his long-term financial goals. Michael never did spend 20%-35% of his income each month because in his current environment, it was not feasible. He could travel but spending money on his base was at a minimum. What Michael did was, start a new savings account for fun spending and allocated the percentages to that account and that account also grew exponentially.

By implementing these strategies and maintaining a disciplined approach to budgeting and saving, individuals can make significant strides towards achieving their financial goals. Remember, every dollar saved today is a step closer to financial freedom and a brighter future. Managing your monthly income to allocate 20%-35% for enjoyment while still paying off debt and saving requires careful planning and discipline.

Here are steps to help you create a budget and manage your finances effectively.

1. Assess Your Financial Situation: Begin by evaluating your current financial status, including your income, expenses, debts, savings and investing. Take stock of all sources of income and identify your fixed expenses, such as rent or mortgage payments, utilities, and insurance.

2. Track Your Spending: Keep track of all your expenses for at least one month to understand where your money is going. This will help you identify areas where you can cut back and allocate more funds towards enjoyment without compromising your financial goals.

3. Set Financial Goals: Define clear financial goals, including paying off debt, building an emergency fund, and saving for future expenses or retirement. Prioritize these goals based on their urgency and importance to your overall financial well-being.

4. Create a Budget: Develop a comprehensive budget that allocates a percentage of your income towards different categories, including debt repayment, savings, necessities, investing and enjoyment. Use the 20-35% guideline to determine how much you can comfortably spend on leisure activities each month. Even if you can't allocate this percentage in the beginning, you can make the necessary adjustments as needed. Remember discipline is your main concern.

5. Prioritize Debt Repayment: If you have outstanding debts, prioritize paying them off as quickly as possible. Allocate a portion of your budget towards debt repayment, focusing on high-interest debts first. Consider using strategies like the debt snowball or debt avalanche method to accelerate repayment.

6. Build an Emergency Fund: Set aside a portion of your income each month to build an emergency fund. Aim to save three to six months' worth of living expenses to cover unexpected costs without resorting to debt.

7. Automate Savings and Debt Payments: Set up automatic transfers to separate accounts for savings, investments, and debt payments. This ensures that you consistently allocate funds towards your financial goals without the need for manual intervention.

8. Cut Back on Expenses: Look for opportunities to reduce discretionary spending and lower your fixed expenses. This could involve renegotiating bills, cutting unnecessary subscriptions, or finding more affordable alternatives for everyday purchases.

9. Monitor and Adjust: Regularly review your budget and track your progress towards your financial goals. Make adjustments as needed to ensure that you stay on track and continue to make progress towards your objectives.

10. Enjoy Responsibly: Once you've allocated funds for debt repayment, savings, investments, and necessities, feel free to enjoy your discretionary income guilt-free. Whether it's dining out, traveling, or pursuing hobbies, prioritize experiences that bring you joy while staying within your budgetary limits.

By following these steps and sticking to your budgeting plan, you can effectively manage your monthly income to allocate 20%-35% for enjoyment while still making progress towards your financial goals. Remember to strike a balance between living in the present and planning for the future and enjoy the journey towards financial freedom.

Mastering the art of budgeting and saving is a crucial step towards achieving financial freedom. By diligently following the steps outlined in this chapter, you can take control of your finances, build a solid foundation for the future, and ultimately realize your dreams of financial independence. Remember, budgeting and saving are not restrictive measures but rather empowering tools that pave the way for a life of abundance and security. These are tools to help you unlock your mind and to start thinking like a millionaire. Stay disciplined, stay focused, and trust in the process.

Next, we will look at another option for saving and budgeting.

The 50/30/20 Rule

As we explore various budgeting rules and percentages for allocating your income towards fixed costs, savings, investments, and discretionary spending, these rules provide structured guidelines for managing your finances effectively and achieving your financial goals. However, it's essential to recognize that there is no one-size-fits-all approach, and ultimately, the choice of budgeting rule depends on your individual circumstances, preferences, and goals.

Whether you choose to follow the rule mentioned earlier or any other variation, what matters most is consistency and discipline in adhering to your chosen budgeting strategy. The 50/30/20 rule is a popular budgeting guideline that suggests allocating your after-tax income into three main categories: needs, wants, and savings & investments (S&I).

Here's how it works based on a $5,000 monthly salary

1. 50% for Needs: Under this rule, 50% of your monthly income, or $2,500 in this case, should be allocated to essential needs such as housing, utilities, groceries, transportation, healthcare, and minimum debt payments. These are expenses that are necessary for your basic living and well-being.

2. 30% for Wants: The next 30% of your income, or $1,500, can be allocated towards discretionary wants or non-essential expenses such as dining out, entertainment, hobbies, vacations, and luxury items. These are expenses that add enjoyment and fulfillment to your life but are not necessary for survival. These can be adjusted based on your style of living but not to exceed 30%.

3. 20% for Savings & Investments: Finally, 20% of your income, or $1,000, should be dedicated to savings and investments. This includes contributions to retirement accounts, emergency savings, debt repayment beyond the minimum payments, and investments in stocks, bonds, mutual funds, or other assets to build wealth over time.

This budgeting rule provides a simple framework for managing your finances and ensuring that you prioritize both short-term enjoyment and long-term financial security. However, as your financial situation evolves, you may find it necessary to adjust the proportions to better suit your needs and goals.

For example, as you begin to minimize your needs and wants and increase your focus on savings and investments, you could shift to a 30/20/50 allocation:

1. 30% for Needs: Reduce your allocation for needs to 30% of your income, or $1,500. This could be achieved by downsizing your living arrangements, cutting back on unnecessary expenses, or refinancing debt to lower monthly payments.

2. 20% for Wants: Maintain the same allocation for wants at 20% of your income, or $1,000. This allows you to continue enjoying discretionary spending while freeing up more funds for savings and investments.

3. 50% for Savings & Investments: Increase your allocation for savings and investments to 50% of your income, or $2,500. This provides a larger pool of funds to contribute towards retirement accounts, emergency savings, debt repayment, and building wealth through investments.

Adjusting the 50/30/20 rule to a 30/20/50 allocation allows you to prioritize savings and investments while still maintaining a reasonable balance between needs and wants. As you progress towards your financial goals, regularly reassessing and fine-tuning your budgeting approach ensures that you stay on track to achieve financial success.

By adopting a "set it and forget it" mentality, you can automate your finances and allocate your cash efficiently without the need for constant manual intervention. This approach allows you to streamline your financial management process and focus on other aspects of your life without worrying about day-to-day money management tasks.

Automating your finances involves setting up automatic transfers and contributions to savings accounts, retirement accounts, and investment accounts according to your chosen budgeting percentages. Additionally, you can use budgeting apps or tools to track your spending, monitor progress towards your financial goals, and adjust as needed.

By embracing a proactive and systematic approach to budgeting and financial planning, you can take control of your finances and make informed decisions that align with your long-term objectives. Whether your goal is to build an emergency fund, save for a down payment on a home, invest for retirement, or simply enjoy discretionary spending, following a consistent budgeting strategy will help you stay on track and achieve financial success. Remember, the key is to find a budgeting rule that works for you and stick to it consistently over time.

In conclusion, Michael's journey towards financial freedom highlights the power of mentorship and self-education in shaping one's financial habits and mindset. While initially not adhering to any specific rules, Michael found guidance and inspiration through mentors and dedicated himself to self-education during his free time, even in the challenging environment of Iraq. While not everyone may have the same opportunities for quiet self-reflection, the accessibility of audiobooks provides a convenient means for continuous learning and personal development.

By leveraging these resources, individuals can empower themselves with knowledge and skills to navigate the complexities of saving, budgeting, and achieving financial independence, regardless of their circumstances. Michael's story serves as a testament to the transformative potential of lifelong learning and the determination to pursue financial success.

As Michael navigated his journey towards financial freedom, a pivotal moment emerged when he was summoned to BALAD Airbase, his Head Quarters base in iraq, to learn about a new technology. This visit held a special significance for Michael, as it presented an opportunity to reunite with Terry, the individual who had initially opened the doors to his transformative journey. Meeting Terry at a coffee shop on the base, Michael embraced him with gratitude, acknowledging the profound impact Terry had made on his life. Over coffee, Terry and Michael engaged in a heartfelt conversation, catching up on the events that had unfolded since their first encounter.

During their discussion, Terry delved into the realm of finances, sharing insights and wisdom on the most effective ways to invest the newfound income that accompanied Michael's job. Intrigued by Terry's advice and motivated by a desire to secure his financial future, Michael listened attentively, absorbing every word. As they parted ways once again, Michael carried with him a wealth of knowledge and inspiration gained from Terry's guidance.

Empowered by Terry's counsel, Michael embarked on a journey of extensive research, delving deep into the world of investing. Armed with newfound understanding and determination, he set his sights on building a robust financial foundation that would pave the way for his long-term prosperity. With Terry's mentorship echoing in his mind, Michael took decisive steps towards realizing his aspirations, poised to unlock the full potential of his financial future.

Chapter 6: Introduction to Investing

In this chapter, we delve into the fascinating world of investing, exploring how individuals like Michael can take control of their financial futures through strategic investment decisions. Michael's journey into investing serves as a testament to the power of self-education and perseverance in mastering the complexities of the stock market.

Michael's foray into investing began with a thirst for knowledge and a desire to grow his wealth. With determination and a commitment to learning, he embarked on a journey of self-education, immersing himself in a plethora of books and research materials on investment strategies and market dynamics. Through diligent study and practice, Michael gradually familiarized himself with various investment techniques, including day trading and option trading.

However, Michael's path to investment success was not without its challenges. Like many novice investors, he experienced setbacks and losses as he navigated the volatile waters of the stock market. Despite initial setbacks, Michael remained undeterred, viewing each loss as a valuable learning opportunity rather than a defeat. Through trial and error, he honed his skills and gained invaluable insights into the intricacies of trading.

As we explore different investment opportunities in this chapter, it's essential to recognize the diverse array of options available to investors like Michael. From traditional investments such as stocks and real estate to alternative assets like commodities and cryptocurrencies, the investment landscape offers a myriad of opportunities for individuals to grow their wealth.

Moreover, we emphasize the importance of diversification and risk management in constructing investment portfolios. Diversifying across various asset classes helps mitigate risk and maximize returns by spreading investments across different sectors and industries. Additionally, prudent risk management practices, such as setting stop-loss orders and adhering to a disciplined investment strategy, are essential for safeguarding against market volatility and unforeseen events.

In essence, this chapter serves as a comprehensive introduction to the world of investing, providing valuable insights and practical guidance for individuals like Michael who aspire to achieve financial success through smart investment decisions. By embracing a diverse range of investment opportunities and adopting sound risk management practices, investors can position themselves for long-term growth and prosperity in the dynamic world of finance.

Through studies, millionaires often employ various investment strategies to grow and preserve their wealth. While individual preferences and circumstances may vary, below you'll learn three of the top ways millionaires invest their money.

How Millionaires Invest:

Stock Market

Millionaires frequently invest in the stock market to capitalize on the potential for long-term capital appreciation. They may purchase individual stocks of established companies with strong growth prospects through mutual funds or exchange-traded funds (ETFs).

Some millionaires also engage in active trading strategies, leveraging their knowledge of the market to buy and sell stocks for short-term gains. However, this approach typically requires significant time, expertise, and risk management skills.

Millionaires may diversify their investment portfolios across various asset classes, including bonds, commodities, alternative investments, and retirement accounts. They often work closely with financial advisors to develop personalized investment strategies aligned with their goals, risk tolerance, and time horizon. By leveraging a combination of investment vehicles and strategies, millionaires aim to optimize returns, mitigate risk, and build a solid foundation.

Real Estate Investing:

Real estate investments are a popular choice among millionaires due to the potential for passive income, appreciation, and portfolio diversification. Millionaires may invest in residential properties, commercial real estate, vacation rentals, or real estate investment trusts (REITs).

Many millionaires leverage financing options such as mortgages to acquire properties and magnify their returns. They may also utilize rental income to cover expenses, pay down debt, and generate additional cash flow.

Entrepreneurial Ventures:

Entrepreneurship offers millionaires the opportunity to build wealth through business ownership and innovation. Many millionaires invest in startups, small businesses, or their own ventures to generate significant returns.

While entrepreneurship can be inherently risky, successful ventures can lead to substantial financial rewards and create lasting value. Millionaires often leverage their expertise, networks, and financial resources to identify promising opportunities and drive business growth.

Business acquisition: Acquiring an existing business can often be a more advantageous route than starting one from scratch. With a business acquisition, you inherit an established customer base, operational infrastructure, and often a proven track record of revenue generation. This reduces the time and resources needed to build brand recognition and develop operational systems. Additionally, you may benefit from synergies between the acquired business and your existing operations, leading to cost savings and revenue growth. Moreover, acquiring a business allows you to mitigate some of the risks associated with launching a new venture, as you have access to historical financial data and insights into the business's performance. Overall, business acquisitions can offer a faster path to profitability and success compared to starting a new business.

These three investment strategies—stock market investments, real estate holdings, and entrepreneurial ventures—offer valuable opportunities for beginners and regular everyday workers to build wealth and achieve financial goals. Investing in the stock market provides accessibility and flexibility, allowing individuals to start with small amounts and gradually grow their portfolios over time. Real estate investments offer tangible assets and the potential for passive income, making them accessible to those interested in property ownership. Entrepreneurial ventures empower individuals to pursue their passions and create wealth through innovative business ideas, regardless of their background or financial status. By exploring these investment avenues and leveraging resources such as education, research, and professional guidance, beginners and hardworking everyday people can embark on a path to financial independence and long-term success.

Beginner Stock Market Investing:

Investing in the stock market can be an exciting and rewarding journey for beginners looking to grow their wealth over time. Before diving into the stock market, it's essential for beginners to understand the basics of investing and familiarize themselves with key concepts.

One of the fundamental principles of investing in the stock market is to buy ownership stakes in companies, known as stocks or shares. Stocks represent a fractional ownership interest in a company, entitling shareholders to a portion of its profits and assets. Beginner investors should start by researching and learning about different types of stocks, including common stocks and preferred stocks.

Common stocks are the most widely traded type of stock and typically offer voting rights and the potential for capital appreciation through price appreciation and dividends. Preferred stocks, on the other hand, often offer fixed dividends but do not usually carry voting rights.

Beginner investors should also understand the concept of risk and reward when investing in stocks. While stocks offer the potential for high returns, they also come with a higher level of risk compared to other investments such as bonds or savings accounts. It's crucial for beginners to develop a well-thought-out investment strategy that aligns with their financial goals, risk tolerance, and time horizon.

Diversification is another key principle of investing in the stock market. By spreading investments across different stocks and industries, beginners can reduce their overall risk exposure. One way to achieve diversification is through investing in mutual funds or exchange-traded funds (ETFs), which pool investors' money to invest in a diversified portfolio of stocks.

Mutual funds and ETFs offer beginners a convenient and cost-effective way to gain exposure to a broad range of stocks without having to pick individual stocks themselves. Before investing in mutual funds or ETFs, beginners should carefully research and compare different funds based on factors such as fees, performance, and investment objectives.

Another important consideration for beginner investors is the concept of asset allocation, which involves dividing investment portfolios among different asset classes such as stocks, bonds, and cash. Asset allocation is a crucial determinant of investment returns and risk levels, and beginners should tailor their asset allocation to their individual financial circumstances and goals.

Beginner investors should also consider the importance of time in the stock market. While short-term fluctuations in stock prices are common, the stock market has historically produced positive returns over the long term of 8%-10% yearly. It's essential for beginners to adopt a long-term perspective and resist the temptation to react impulsively to short-term market movements.

Dollar-cost averaging is a strategy that can help beginner investors navigate market volatility by investing a fixed amount of money at regular intervals, regardless of market conditions. By dollar-cost averaging, beginners can potentially lower the average cost per share of their investments over time and reduce the impact of market fluctuations on their portfolio.

Another key concept for beginner investors to understand is the importance of conducting thorough research and due diligence before investing in individual stocks. Researching stocks involves analyzing company financials, industry trends, competitive positioning, management quality, and other relevant factors to assess the investment potential of a particular stock.

Beginner investors should also consider seeking guidance from financial advisors or experienced investors to help them navigate the complexities of the stock market and develop a sound investment strategy. Building a diversified portfolio of individual stocks requires careful consideration of factors such as risk tolerance, investment goals, and time horizon.

Beginners can start by investing in well-established companies with strong fundamentals and a track record of consistent earnings and dividend growth. Dividend-paying stocks can be particularly attractive to beginner investors seeking regular income streams and potential capital appreciation over time.

When selecting individual stocks, beginners should also pay attention to valuation metrics such as price-to-earnings (P/E) ratio, price-to-book (P/B) ratio, and dividend yield to assess whether a stock is undervalued or overvalued relative to its peers and the broader market. Beginner investors should be cautious of speculative or highly volatile stocks that may carry a higher level of risk and uncertainty.

Risk management is a critical aspect of successful investing in the stock market. Beginners should avoid investing more than they can afford to lose and consider setting stop-loss orders to limit potential losses. It's essential for beginner investors to stay informed about market developments, economic indicators, and company news that may impact stock prices.

Beginner investors can use a variety of resources to stay informed, including financial news websites, investment forums, and educational materials provided by brokerage firms and investment platforms. Patience and discipline are virtues that beginner investors should cultivate when investing in the stock market. Building wealth through investing takes time and requires a long-term commitment to staying the course despite short-term market fluctuations.

Beginners should resist the urge to chase hot stock tips or follow the herd mentality, as such strategies can often lead to poor investment decisions and disappointing outcomes. Instead, beginner investors should focus on building a well-diversified portfolio of high-quality stocks and holding onto them for the long term, allowing the power of compounding to work in their favor.

Rebalancing is an essential aspect of portfolio management that beginner investors should incorporate into their investment strategy. Rebalancing involves periodically adjusting the allocation of assets in a portfolio to maintain desired risk levels and investment objectives.

By rebalancing regularly, beginners can ensure that their investment portfolios remain aligned with their financial goals and risk tolerance, even as market conditions change over time.

Tax efficiency is another important consideration for beginner investors, as taxes can erode investment returns over time. Beginners should familiarize themselves with tax-efficient investment strategies, such as investing in tax-advantaged accounts like IRAs and 401(k) plans.

When investing in individual stocks, beginners should consider the tax implications of buying and selling stocks, including capital gains taxes, and holding period requirements. Beginner investors can also explore tax-loss harvesting strategies to offset capital gains and reduce their overall tax liability.

Risk tolerance is a crucial factor that beginner investors should assess before diving into the stock market. Risk tolerance refers to an investor's ability and willingness to withstand fluctuations in the value of their investments without panicking or making impulsive decisions. Beginner investors should conduct a thorough risk assessment to determine their risk tolerance level and tailor their investment strategy accordingly.

Risk tolerance is influenced by various factors, including age, financial goals, investment experience, time horizon, and personal circumstances. Younger investors with a longer time horizon and higher risk tolerance may be more inclined to invest in riskier assets such as stocks, while older investors nearing retirement may prefer a more conservative investment approach focused on capital preservation. To assess their risk tolerance, beginner investors can use risk tolerance questionnaires and online tools provided by financial institutions and investment platforms. These tools typically ask questions about investment preferences, financial goals, time horizon, and attitude towards risk to help investors determine an appropriate asset allocation.

Beginner investors should also consider their capacity for risk, which refers to their financial ability to withstand investment losses without jeopardizing their long-term financial security. Investors with higher income levels, stable employment, and ample savings may have a higher capacity for risk compared to those with lower income levels and fewer financial resources. It's essential for beginner investors to strike a balance between risk and return when constructing their investment portfolios. While taking on too much risk can expose investors to potential losses, being too conservative may limit their potential for long-term growth and wealth accumulation.

One way to manage risk in the stock market is through diversification, which involves spreading investments across different asset classes, industries, and geographic regions to reduce the impact of any single investment or market downturn on the overall portfolio. Diversification can help beginner investors mitigate risk and achieve more consistent returns over time by offsetting losses in one area of the portfolio with gains in another.

Beginner investors can achieve diversification by investing in a mix of stocks, bonds, cash equivalents, and alternative assets such as real estate investment trusts (REITs), commodities, and precious metals.

Exchange-traded funds (ETFs) and mutual funds offer beginner investors a convenient and cost-effective way to gain exposure to diversified portfolios of stocks and bonds without having to pick individual securities themselves. When selecting ETFs and mutual funds, beginner investors should consider factors such as fees, performance history, investment objectives, and underlying holdings to ensure they align with their financial goals and risk tolerance.

By adopting a disciplined investment approach, staying informed about market developments, and focusing on long-term goals, beginner investors can navigate the stock market with confidence and build wealth over time.

Real Estate Investing for Beginners:

Whether you're a seasoned investor looking to diversify your portfolio or a beginner eager to explore new avenues of wealth creation, real estate offers a wide range of investment opportunities to suit many of your goals and preferences.

Real estate investing has long been heralded as one of the most reliable and lucrative ways to build wealth over time. Unlike stocks, bonds, or other traditional investments, real estate provides tangible assets that can generate passive income, appreciate in value, and offer tax advantages, making it an attractive option for investors seeking long-term financial security.

If you're a beginner to real estate investing, we'll explore the fundamentals of the real estate market, the various investment strategies available to investors, and the key principles and best practices that can help you succeed in this dynamic and rewarding field. Whether you're interested in rental properties, fix-and-flip projects, commercial real estate, or other investment opportunities, these steps will provide you with the knowledge and tools you need to get started on your journey to real estate riches.

Throughout the steps, we'll cover essential topics such as market analysis, property selection, financing options, risk management, and property management, giving you a comprehensive understanding of the real estate investment process from start to finish. We'll also delve into advanced strategies, emerging trends, and innovative approaches to real estate investing, equipping you with the insights and expertise needed to navigate today's ever-changing market landscape.

But before we dive into the specifics of real estate investing, it's important to understand why real estate has long been considered a cornerstone of wealth creation and financial freedom. Unlike other investment vehicles that may be subject to market volatility or economic downturns, real estate offers a unique combination of stability, predictability, and potential for growth that can help investors weather even the toughest of economic climates.

From rental properties that provide consistent cash flow to fix-and-flip projects that offer substantial returns on investment, real estate offers a variety of investment strategies that can be tailored to suit your individual goals, risk tolerance, and investment timeline. Whether you're looking to generate passive income, build equity over time, or achieve financial independence, real estate investing offers a wealth of opportunities for investors of all backgrounds and experience levels.

So, whether you're a novice investor eager to dip your toes into the world of real estate or a seasoned pro looking to expand your portfolio, join us as we embark on an exciting journey into the world of real estate investing. With the right knowledge, mindset, and strategies, you too can harness the power of real estate to achieve your financial goals and create the life of your dreams.

Michael's foray into real estate investing began unexpectedly, sparked by a realization while he was overseas working. Having purchased his home years prior under the guidance of his father and influenced by Alonzo's wisdom, Michael hadn't initially considered the potential of his property beyond being a place to live. However, through self-learning he opened his eyes to the possibility of turning his home into a rental property.

Upon learning about this opportunity, Michael wasted no time in exploring the idea further. He recognized the potential to generate additional income by renting out his property while he was away, an idea that hadn't crossed his mind before. With some research and guidance, Michael took the plunge and transformed his home into a rental property. A property management company handled everything for Michael for a small 10% fee on the rental income, but this would ensure all Michael had to do was sit and receive a payment each month without doing anything. Michael was able to start his own LLC (Limited Liability Company) to manage his property. Over time, Michael added to his portfolio of properties that his company managed.

The decision proved to be a game-changer for Michael. Not only did he start earning rental income, but he also experienced the benefits of equity build-up as his tenants paid down the mortgage. Moreover, he enjoyed savings on various expenses, including utilities and yard maintenance, and other upkeep expenses as these responsibilities now fell on the renters.

This newfound stream of income was a revelation for Michael. It provided him with an introduction to the world of real estate investing and opened his eyes to the potential of leveraging his property to build wealth. What started as a simple decision to rent out his home turned into a significant source of passive income and financial security.

Through this experience, Michael learned firsthand the power of real estate investing and the many advantages it offered. From generating passive income to building equity and enjoying tax benefits, he discovered the wealth-building potential of owning rental properties. This realization ignited a passion for real estate investing within Michael, prompting him to explore further opportunities in the field.

Indeed, Michael's journey into real estate investing serves as a testament to the transformative power of seizing opportunities and thinking outside the box. By leveraging his existing assets and exploring new avenues for income generation, he unlocked a path to financial freedom and opened doors to a brighter financial future.

Entrepreneurial Ventures for Beginners:

Non-business owners can achieve entrepreneurship by starting their own business, regardless of their current employment status. One way to start a business is by identifying a market need or gap and developing a product or service to address it. This could involve leveraging existing skills, hobbies, or passions to create a business idea that aligns with personal interests and expertise.

Another approach is to explore franchising opportunities, where individuals can invest in established business models and benefit from brand recognition, support, and proven systems. Franchising offers a lower barrier to entry compared to starting a business from scratch and can be an attractive option for those seeking a turnkey solution.

Additionally, individuals can pursue freelancing or consulting opportunities in their area of expertise, offering services such as graphic design, writing, marketing, or coaching. Freelancing allows individuals to work independently, set their own rates, and build a client base while gradually transitioning into full-time entrepreneurship.

For those interested in e-commerce, starting an online store, or selling products through platforms like Etsy, eBay, or Amazon can be a viable option. E-commerce businesses require minimal upfront investment and offer flexibility in terms of product selection, marketing strategies, and scalability.

Furthermore, aspiring entrepreneurs can explore the gig economy by driving for ride-sharing services, delivering groceries, or providing on-demand services through platforms like TaskRabbit or Fiverr. These opportunities offer flexibility, instant income, and the potential to transition into full-fledged businesses over time.

Regardless of the chosen path, starting a business requires careful planning, research, and dedication. It's essential to conduct market research, develop a solid business plan, and seek mentorship or guidance from experienced entrepreneurs or business professionals. By taking calculated risks, leveraging resources, and embracing opportunities for growth, non-business owners can embark on the journey of entrepreneurship and work towards achieving financial freedom and independence. It only takes one question asked to spark your business ventures.

Start an LLC (Limited Liability Company)

Starting an LLC (Limited Liability Company) can be a great first step into entrepreneurship due to its simplicity and flexibility. Forming an LLC provides personal liability protection, separating your personal assets from those of the business. This shields your personal assets from business debts and liabilities, offering peace of mind as you embark on your entrepreneurial journey. Additionally, LLCs offer flexibility in management structure and tax treatment, allowing you to choose how the business is managed and taxed. The process of starting an LLC is relatively straightforward and can often be completed online with minimal paperwork and low cost. Typically, you'll need to choose a unique name for your LLC, file articles of organization with the state, and create an operating agreement outlining how the business will be managed. Once these steps are completed and any necessary fees are paid, your LLC will be officially formed, and you can begin conducting business under its umbrella. Overall, starting an LLC is an accessible and efficient way to establish your business and lay the foundation for future growth and success.

Differences Between Stock Investing and Real Estate Investing:

Stock investing involves purchasing shares of publicly traded companies, thereby acquiring ownership in those companies. Investors buy stocks with the expectation that the company's value will increase over time, allowing them to sell their shares at a profit. In contrast, real estate investing involves purchasing physical properties such as houses, apartments, or commercial buildings with the intention of generating rental income or capital appreciation. One key difference between stock investing and real estate investing lies in the underlying assets. Stocks represent ownership stakes in companies, while real estate investments involve tangible assets such as land and buildings.

Another distinction between stock investing and real estate investing is the level of liquidity. Stocks are highly liquid investments, meaning they can be easily bought and sold on public stock exchanges within seconds. Real estate, on the other hand, is relatively illiquid, as it can take weeks or even months to sell a property and convert it into cash. Stock investing offers investors the opportunity to diversify their portfolios across various industries and sectors, providing exposure to a broad range of companies and markets. Real estate investing allows investors to diversify their portfolios by investing in different types of properties, locations, and asset classes such as residential, commercial, or industrial real estate.

Stock investing typically requires less initial capital compared to real estate investing. Investors can buy stocks with as little as a few dollars, making it accessible to a wide range of investors. In contrast, real estate investing often requires a significant upfront investment, including down payments, closing costs, and ongoing maintenance expenses. Both stock investing and real estate investing offer the potential for passive income through dividends or rental income. Dividends are payments made by companies to their shareholders, while rental income is generated from leasing out properties to tenants.

Stock investing provides investors with the flexibility to buy and sell shares quickly, allowing them to capitalize on short-term market trends and opportunities. Real estate investing, on the other hand, typically involves longer holding periods, as properties may take time to appreciate in value and generate rental income. Stock investors can leverage financial instruments such as options, futures, and margin accounts to enhance their returns or hedge against risks. Real estate investors can use leverage by taking out mortgages to finance property purchases, thereby increasing their potential returns but also their risk exposure.

Stock investing offers investors the opportunity to participate in corporate governance through voting rights and shareholder activism. Real estate investing provides investors with direct control over property management and decision-making, such as setting rental rates, screening tenants, and making property improvements. Both stock investing and real estate investing carry inherent risks and uncertainties. Stock prices can be highly volatile, fluctuating in response to market conditions, economic indicators, and company performance. Real estate values can also fluctuate based on factors such as local market dynamics, interest rates, and demographic trends.

Stock investors can easily access market information, company financials, and investment research through online platforms, financial news outlets, and brokerage firms. Real estate investors rely on market data, property listings, and industry reports to make informed investment decisions. Stock investing offers investors the opportunity for capital appreciation, as stock prices can rise over time in response to company growth, profitability, and market demand. Real estate investing provides investors with the potential for capital appreciation through property appreciation and value-added improvements.

Stock investors can invest in a wide range of asset classes, including equities, bonds, commodities, and currencies, through diversified investment vehicles such as mutual funds, exchange-traded funds (ETFs), and index funds. Real estate investors can invest in various types of properties, including single-family homes, multi-family apartments, office buildings, retail centers, and industrial warehouses.

Stock investing allows investors to benefit from the expertise of professional fund managers and financial advisors who actively manage investment portfolios and provide investment advice. Real estate investing offers investors the opportunity to leverage the expertise of property managers, real estate agents, and contractors who specialize in property management, leasing, and renovations.

Stock investing offers investors the flexibility to adjust their investment strategies and portfolios quickly in response to changing market conditions and economic trends. Real estate investing typically requires longer-term commitments and may involve more complex transactions, such as property acquisitions, renovations, and leasing agreements.

Stock investing provides investors with access to global markets and international diversification opportunities, allowing them to invest in companies headquartered in different countries and regions. Real estate investing offers investors the opportunity to invest in local, regional, national or international real estate markets, depending on their investment preferences and objectives.

Both stock investing and real estate investing can provide tax benefits to investors. Stock investors may benefit from tax advantages such as capital gains tax rates and qualified dividend tax rates. Real estate investors can take advantage of tax deductions such as mortgage interest, property taxes, depreciation, and operating expenses.

Stock investing requires investors to monitor market developments, company performance, and economic indicators regularly to make informed investment decisions and adjust their portfolios accordingly. Real estate investing involves actively managing properties, overseeing tenant relationships, and addressing maintenance issues to maximize returns and minimize risks.

Stock investing offers investors the potential for high returns but also comes with higher volatility and risk. Real estate investing provides investors with the opportunity for steady, predictable income but may involve higher initial costs and ongoing management responsibilities.

Ultimately, the choice between stock investing and real estate investing depends on factors such as investment goals, risk tolerance, time horizon, and personal preferences. Both asset classes offer unique benefits and challenges, and diversifying across both stocks and real estate can provide investors with.

Chapter 7: Getting Started in the Stock Market

In Michael's journey of investing in the stock market, he started with a modest account of around $500 on TD Ameritrade. Eager to grow his account, he ventured into day trading, buying, and selling stocks within the same trading day. However, Michael quickly learned that day trading came with its challenges, especially with a small account size. His frequent trades triggered restrictions on his account, preventing him from executing more trades. It was a lesson learned the hard way—day trading required a minimum account value of $25,000 to avoid such limitations.

Undeterred by setbacks, Michael recognized the need for a more conservative approach. He delved into studying graphs and learning the technical aspects of the stock market, seeking to refine his trading strategies. Along the way, Michael sought advice from colleagues who shared insights on long-term trading and incorporating occasional short-term trades to build his account steadily.

One of the most valuable lessons Michael learned was patience. In an environment where many seek quick wins and instant gratification, Michael realized that success in the stock market often requires a long-term perspective. While some traders may thrive on daily fluctuations, the stock market's true potential lies in accumulating wealth over time through strategic investments and disciplined decision-making.

Through trial and error, Michael discovered the importance of managing risk and staying grounded in his investment approach. He embraced the notion that the stock market is a journey, not a sprint, and that consistent, informed decisions yield more sustainable results in the long run. By cultivating patience and focusing on continuous learning and improvement, Michael gradually navigated the complexities of the stock market and paved his path but following guidelines and certain rules anyone can become successful in trading in the stock market. We will look at some ways to start your journey.

When starting your investing journey with a brokerage company, it's important to follow some basic steps to ensure you build a strong foundation for your portfolio. The first step is to open a brokerage account, where you can buy and sell investments. Once you've opened your account, you'll need to fund it with money to invest. With $1000 to start, you can begin by diversifying your portfolio across different asset classes and investment types.

To begin, allocate $500 to establish your foundation with two Exchange-Traded Funds (ETFs): VOO (Vanguard S&P 500 ETF) and VFV (Vanguard S&P 500 Index ETF). These ETFs provide broad exposure to the stock market, offering a solid base for your portfolio.

Next, allocate $250 to invest in two growth stocks: KO (The Coca-Cola Company) and NKE (Nike, Inc.). These stocks are considered income stocks, as they have a history of paying dividends and offer stability and steady growth potential over time.

For your growth stocks, allocate another $250 to invest in two dividend-paying stocks: AMZN (Amazon.com, Inc.) and AAPL (Apple Inc.). These stocks are known for their strong growth potential and consistent dividend payments, providing a source of income while also offering the opportunity for capital appreciation.

Finally, allocate $250 to invest in two more diversified options: QQQ (Invesco QQQ Trust), which tracks the performance of the Nasdaq-100 Index and focuses on technology stocks, and SCHD (Schwab US Dividend Equity ETF), which invests in stable companies that pay dividends. These investments add further diversification to your portfolio and help mitigate risk.

By diversifying your portfolio across different asset classes and investment types, you can build a solid foundation for long-term growth and wealth accumulation. Remember to stay focused on your investment goals, and don't make investing complicated. With time and experience, you can continue to learn and refine your investment strategy to achieve financial success.

What is Diversifying your Portfolio

Diversifying your portfolio is crucial for managing risk and maximizing returns over the long term. By spreading your investments across different asset classes, sectors, and geographic regions, you can reduce the impact of any single investment's performance on your overall portfolio. This means that if one investment underperforms, others may still perform well, helping to mitigate losses.

Additionally, diversification can provide exposure to different market conditions and economic cycles. For example, when one sector is experiencing a downturn, another sector may be performing strongly, helping to balance out overall portfolio returns.

Contributing a certain percentage of your income to your portfolio each month is also important for building wealth over time. Consistent contributions, regardless of market fluctuations, allow you to take advantage of dollar-cost averaging. This strategy involves investing a fixed amount of money at regular intervals, which can help smooth out the impact of market volatility over time and potentially lower the average cost of your investments.

Moreover, regular contributions help instill discipline and consistency in your investment approach, ensuring that you continue to build your portfolio steadily over time. Whether you're investing in stocks, bonds, mutual funds, or ETFs, making regular contributions can help you achieve your long-term financial goals while managing risk effectively.

Overall, the combination of diversification and consistent contributions can help you build a resilient portfolio that is better positioned to weather market fluctuations and generate sustainable wealth over the long term.

Easiest way to Start investing

Another effective way to start investing and probably the easiest is by taking advantage of your company's 401(k) match plan. Many employers offer this benefit to encourage employees to save for retirement. Investing in your company's 401k plan only requires you to do one thing and that is setup your automatic deductions and the company will handle your investing for you through their batch of stocks. They will also diversify your account automatically and this requires little to no effort from you. Here's how it works:

I. Employer Match: With a 401(k) match plan, your employer agrees to match a portion of your contributions to your retirement account, up to a certain percentage of your salary. For example, your employer might offer to match 50% of your contributions, up to 6% of your salary. This means that if you contribute 6% of your salary to your 401(k), your employer will contribute an additional 3%.

2. Free Money: Taking advantage of your company's 401(k) match is like getting free money. By contributing enough to your 401(k) to receive the full match from your employer, you're essentially doubling your investment right from the start.

3. Tax Benefits: Contributions to a traditional 401(k) are made with pre-tax dollars, which means you can lower your taxable income for the year. This can result in immediate tax savings, as well as tax-deferred growth on your investments until you withdraw the money in retirement.

4. Automatic Contributions: Many 401(k) plans offer the option to set up automatic contributions from your paycheck, making it easy to save consistently over time. This helps instill discipline in your saving and investing habits, ensuring that you're building a nest egg for your future.

5. Long-Term Growth: Investing in your company's 401(k) match plan allows you to benefit from the power of compounding over time. By regularly contributing to your retirement account and taking advantage of your employer's match, you can build a substantial portfolio that grows steadily over the course of your career.

Overall, using your company's 401(k) match plan is a smart and effective way to start investing for the future. It provides you with the opportunity to save and invest for retirement while also taking advantage of valuable employer benefits and tax advantages.

Michael's decision to prioritize paying off high-interest debt before contributing to his company's 401(k) match plan demonstrates a wise financial strategy. High-interest debt, such as credit card debt, can significantly erode potential investment gains over time due to its hefty monthly interest rates. By focusing on paying off this debt first, Michael is effectively freeing up more money in the long run that would have otherwise gone towards interest payments.

Eliminating high-interest debt is crucial because it allows individuals to redirect those funds towards investments that can generate higher returns over time. Once the debt is paid off, Michael can then allocate those freed-up funds towards contributing to his company's 401(k) match plan. By taking advantage of the employer match, Michael is effectively doubling his investment right from the start, providing a significant boost to his retirement savings.

Moreover, by eliminating high-interest debt, individuals can reduce financial stress and improve

their overall financial health. Without the burden of debt weighing them down, they can focus on building a solid financial foundation and securing their future. By taking proactive steps to eliminate debt and prioritize saving for retirement, individuals like Michael can set themselves up for long-term financial success and achieve their goals with confidence.

Here are ten top brokerage firms for investing:
• Charles Schwab
• Fidelity Investments
• TD Ameritrade
• E*TRADE
• Vanguard
• Merrill Edge (Bank of America)
• Interactive Brokers
• Robinhood
• Ally Invest
• SoFi Invest

5 Types of 401k account types

The term "401(k) account types" typically refers to different features or options within a 401(k) plan rather than distinct types of accounts. However, I can provide information on five common features or options found in 401(k) plans:

1. Traditional 401(k): Contributions are made with pre-tax dollars, reducing taxable income in the current year. Withdrawals in retirement are taxed as ordinary income.

2. Roth 401(k): Contributions are made with after-tax dollars, so qualified withdrawals in retirement, including earnings, are tax-free.

3. Safe Harbor 401(k): A Safe Harbor 401(k) plan offers simplified rules and nondiscrimination testing requirements by requiring the employer to make mandatory contributions to employee accounts, either through matching or non-elective contributions.

4. Solo 401(k) (or Individual 401(k): Designed for self-employed individuals or small business owners with no employees other than a spouse, a Solo 401(k) allows for higher contribution limits and greater control over investment options.

5. SIMPLE 401(k) (Savings Incentive Match Plan for Employees): Available to small businesses with 100 or fewer employees, SIMPLE 401(k) plans offer simplified administration and lower contribution limits compared to traditional 401(k) plans. Employers are required to make contributions either through matching or non-elective contributions.

What if you leave your company?

When leaving a company, you have the option to rollover your 401(k) account to an Individual Retirement Account (IRA) with your own brokerage firm. This rollover process allows you to maintain control over your retirement savings and continue investing in a tax-advantaged account. Here's how it works:

1. Open an IRA: First, you'll need to open an IRA account with a brokerage firm of your choice. You can choose between a Traditional IRA or a Roth IRA, depending on your preference for tax treatment.

2. Initiate the Rollover: Contact your 401(k) plan administrator and request a direct rollover of your account balance to your newly opened IRA. This ensures that the funds are transferred directly from your 401(k) account to your IRA without any tax implications or penalties.

3. Choose Investments: Once the rollover is complete and the funds are deposited into your IRA, you can start investing in ETFs and mutual funds of your choice. By selecting investments with growth potential and diversification, you can maximize your returns and continue to benefit from compound interest over time.

4. Contribute Regularly: With your rollover IRA set up, you can continue to contribute to the account up to the maximum annual contribution limit allowed by the IRS. As of 2022, the annual contribution limit for IRAs is $6,000 for individuals under age 50 and $7,000 for individuals age 50 and older (catch-up contributions). By the time you read this book these contributions could have increased so check with your brokerage or financial advisor.

5. Monitor and Rebalance: Regularly monitor your investments and adjust your portfolio as needed to maintain diversification and alignment with your long-term financial goals. Rebalance your portfolio periodically to ensure that your asset allocation remains on track.

By rolling over your 401(k) to an IRA with your own brokerage firm, you retain control over your retirement savings and gain access to a wider range of investment options. By continuing to contribute regularly and investing wisely, you can maximize your growth potential and secure a comfortable retirement.

For beginners venturing into stock market investing, conducting thorough research, constructing a diversified portfolio, and managing risks are essential steps to navigate the complexities of the financial markets. Here's a guide to help beginners get started:

I. Researching Stocks:

- Start by understanding basic financial concepts and terminology related to stocks, such as earnings per share (EPS), price-to-earnings ratio (P/E ratio), and dividend yield.
- Utilize reputable financial websites, such as Yahoo Finance, Bloomberg, or CNBC, to research and analyze potential stocks. Look for information on company fundamentals, financial performance, industry trends, and analyst ratings.
- Consider reading annual reports, quarterly earnings reports, and press releases issued by companies to gain insights into their operations, growth prospects, and competitive positioning.
- Evaluate qualitative factors such as the company's business model, management team, competitive advantages, and future growth potential.

2. Building a Portfolio:

- Adopt a diversified approach by investing in a mix of stocks across different industries, sectors, and market capitalizations. Diversification helps spread risk and reduces the impact of any single stock's performance on your overall portfolio.
- Determine your investment objectives, risk tolerance, and time horizon to tailor your portfolio to your financial goals and personal preferences.
- Consider allocating a portion of your portfolio to index funds or exchange-traded funds (ETFs) to gain exposure to broad market indices, providing instant diversification at a lower cost.
- Regularly review and rebalance your portfolio to maintain your desired asset allocation and adjust to changes in market conditions or your investment objectives.

3. Mitigating Risks:

- Conduct thorough due diligence before investing in any stock, analyzing both the company's strengths and weaknesses, as well as external factors that may impact its performance.
- Practice risk management by setting clear investment criteria and establishing stop-loss orders to limit potential losses on individual positions.

- Avoid overconcentration in any single stock or sector, as this increases your exposure to specific risks. Aim for a well-diversified portfolio with a mix of assets.

- Stay informed about market developments, economic indicators, and geopolitical events that may influence stock prices and overall market sentiment.

- Consider incorporating defensive strategies such as hedging techniques or investing in defensive sectors like utilities or consumer staples during periods of market uncertainty.

By following these guidelines and continuously learning and adapting to market dynamics, beginners can embark on their stock market investing journey with greater confidence and a higher likelihood of long-term success.

After Michael mastered the intricacies of the stock market, he decided to take his trading endeavors to the next level. With a newfound confidence in his abilities, Michael funded his trading account with a little over $25,000, meeting the minimum requirement for day trading without restrictions. Now unrestricted by trade limits, Michael could execute trades as frequently as he desired.

Determined to capitalize on his newfound freedom, Michael dedicated all his spare time to researching stocks, analyzing market trends, and refining his trading strategies. Long before the opening bell rang on Wall Street, Michael was meticulously prepared, armed with a wealth of knowledge and a keen eye for profitable opportunities.

In the first 6-8 months of his intensive trading regimen, Michael's account swelled to over $80,000, a testament to his disciplined approach and shrewd decision-making. To achieve such remarkable growth, Michael leveraged the power of a margin account.

A margin account is a brokerage account that allows investors to borrow funds from the broker to purchase securities. With a margin account, traders can amplify their buying power, potentially magnifying their profits. However, margin trading also introduces increased risk, as traders may incur losses exceeding their initial investment.

As Michael's success in the stock market became widely known, he began sharing his expertise with others, offering insights and guidance on navigating the complexities of trading. Recognizing an opportunity to leverage his knowledge for profit, Michael devised a brilliant plan: he would offer to manage trading accounts for others, charging a fee equivalent to 15% of the monthly gains.

With unwavering confidence in his ability to deliver consistent returns, Michael wasted no time in putting his plan into action. Before long, he found himself not only managing his own account but also overseeing the investments of three additional clients.

As Michael expanded his trading endeavors to manage multiple accounts, he found himself juggling various responsibilities. While he couldn't devote all his time to his personal trading account, he devised a clever solution: charging a 15% management fee for each account he oversaw. This arrangement allowed him to generate steady income while leveraging his expertise to grow his clients' investments. With each successful trade, Michael solidified his reputation as a skilled trader and financial advisor, transforming his passion for the stock market into a lucrative business venture of his own.

With his streamlined approach to trading, Michael capitalized on the volatile morning market, executing swift trades within the first 15 minutes of the opening bell. By strategically timing his trades, Michael could effortlessly pocket $300 in profits for himself and his clients, capitalizing on fleeting opportunities in the market's initial flurry of activity.

To maintain discipline and avoid succumbing to greed, Michael implemented a series of self-imposed guidelines. He plastered sticky notes on his monitor, each bearing a simple yet powerful mantra: "Don't be greedy." Reminding himself to adhere to his predetermined goals, Michael focused on taking profits when opportunities arose, adhering to his targets of 10%-20% gains.

These sticky notes served as constant reminders to stay disciplined and stick to his trading plan, even in the face of enticing prospects for larger profits. By adhering to his principles and resisting the temptation to deviate from his strategy, Michael safeguarded his investments and ensured consistent returns for both him and his clients.

As Michael's stock market trading days continued, a significant change disrupted his routine: he was transferred to a new base to provide crucial technical support. This relocation posed a challenge for Michael, as his expertise was urgently required to revitalize the struggling site. Amidst the demands of his new assignment, Michael found it increasingly difficult to engage in his usual trading activities.

The transition to the new base brought with it additional stressors, as the heightened security risks and frequent attacks made safety a top priority. With bombings and mortar rounds posing constant threats, Michael's focus shifted from trading to ensuring his own well-being and remaining vigilant in the face of danger.

As the demands of his new role consumed his time and energy, Michael realized that he could no longer fulfill his obligations to his trading clients. With a heavy heart, he reached out to them, explaining the circumstances and regretfully informing them of his inability to continue managing their accounts.

Undeterred by this setback, Michael pivoted his investment strategy, shifting his focus from active trading to long-term investments. Recognizing the value of consistent, steady growth, he directed his profits and account earnings towards building a portfolio of long-term stocks.

To streamline this new approach, Michael implemented automatic contributions, mirroring the system he had previously established for his other long-term trading accounts. By automating his investment process, Michael ensured that his money continued working for him, even as his attention was diverted to his responsibilities at the new base.

Though the transition brought its share of challenges and uncertainties, Michael remained steadfast in his commitment to financial growth and stability. Despite the limitations imposed by his circumstances, he adapted his investment strategy to align with his current reality, laying the foundation for continued success in the ever-changing landscape of the stock market.

Chapter 8: Real Estate Investment Strategies

Investing in real estate offers a multitude of benefits, ranging from potential long-term wealth accumulation to the generation of passive income streams. One of the primary advantages of real estate investment is its ability to provide steady cash flow through rental income. Additionally, real estate investments have historically exhibited favorable appreciation rates, allowing investors to build equity over time. Diversification is another key benefit, as real estate often behaves differently than other asset classes, thereby mitigating overall portfolio risk. Real estate investments can also serve as a hedge against inflation, as property values and rental income tend to increase with rising prices.

Investing in real estate grants investors greater control over their investments compared to other asset classes. Unlike stocks or bonds, where performance is largely dependent on market conditions, real estate investors have the autonomy to influence property value through strategic improvements and renovations. Real estate investments also offer tax advantages, including deductions for mortgage interest, property taxes, and depreciation, which can help reduce taxable income.

There are several approaches to property investment, each with its own set of advantages and considerations. One common strategy is buy-and-hold investing, where investors purchase properties with the intention of holding them long-term to generate rental income and potential appreciation. Fix-and-flip investing involves purchasing distressed properties, renovating them, and selling them for a profit in a relatively short period. Michael took the buy and hold approach because it required less effort. You buy a property that's ready for rent. Fix-and-flip requires strategy, planning, money, and lots of time. You also need a team of construction workers to complete the rehabilitation of the property.

Real estate crowdfunding platforms allow investors to pool their funds to invest in larger properties, offering opportunities for diversification and passive income without the responsibilities of property management. REITs (Real Estate Investment Trusts) provide another avenue for real estate investment, allowing investors to purchase shares in companies that own and manage income-generating properties. Finally, short-term rental investing, often facilitated through platforms like Airbnb, enables investors to generate income from vacation or short-term rentals.

Regardless of the chosen approach, successful real estate investing requires thorough research, due diligence, and a clear investment strategy tailored to individual goals and risk tolerance. By leveraging the benefits of real estate investment and adopting a disciplined approach, investors can build wealth, generate passive income, and achieve financial independence over time.

For individuals who haven't yet purchased their first home but are interested in real estate investment, there are still several accessible avenues to get started. As we mentioned previously, one easy option is to begin by investing in real estate investment trusts (REITs). REITs are companies that own, operate, or finance income-generating real estate across various sectors, such as residential, commercial, or industrial properties. Investing in REITs provides exposure to the real estate market without the need for direct property ownership, making it an ideal starting point for beginners.

Another approach is to explore real estate crowdfunding platforms. These platforms allow individuals to invest in real estate projects alongside other investors, pooling funds to finance properties such as residential developments, commercial buildings, or rental properties. Real estate crowdfunding offers opportunities for diversification and passive income, with investment minimums often lower than traditional property purchases. Be sure to vet who you'll be investing with.

Additionally, prospective investors can consider investing in real estate through real estate investment groups or partnerships. These arrangements involve pooling resources with other investors to purchase and manage properties collectively. Real estate investment groups typically require a smaller financial commitment than sole ownership, making them more accessible to beginners.

Furthermore, aspiring investors can explore purchasing shares of publicly traded homebuilders or real estate development companies. By investing in these companies through the stock market, individuals can gain exposure to the real estate sector while benefiting from liquidity and diversification.

Lastly, individuals can educate themselves on real estate investing principles through books, online courses, or seminars. Building a foundational understanding of real estate fundamentals, market trends, and investment strategies is crucial for making informed investment decisions and navigating the complexities of the real estate market.

Overall, while not yet owning a home, individuals can still embark on their real estate investment journey through many avenues. By starting small and gradually expanding their investment portfolio, aspiring investors can begin building wealth through real estate even without direct property ownership.

Buying Your First Home:

Buying your first single-family property can be an exciting but complex process. Here are steps to guide you through the process:

1. Assess Your Finances: Evaluate your financial situation, including your savings, income, credit score, and debt-to-income ratio. Determine how much you can afford to spend on a property and secure pre-approval for a mortgage if necessary.

2. Define Your Criteria: Consider your housing needs, preferences, and budget. Determine the location, size, amenities, and features you desire in a single-family property. Make a list of your must-haves and nice-to-haves to guide your search.

3. Research the Market: Research the real estate market in your desired location. Look at property prices, trends, and inventory levels. Understand factors such as neighborhood dynamics, school districts, crime rates, and amenities that may influence your decision.

4. Find a Real Estate Agent: Hire a reputable real estate agent who specializes in the local market. An experienced agent can help you navigate the buying process, identify suitable properties, negotiate offers, and handle paperwork.

5. Start House Hunting: Begin searching for single-family properties that meet your criteria. Utilize online listing platforms, attend open houses, and work closely with your real estate agent to identify potential properties. Visit properties in person to assess their condition, layout, and suitability.

6. Conduct Due Diligence: Once you find a property of interest, conduct thorough due diligence. Review property disclosures, inspection reports, title documents, and zoning regulations. Consider hiring a professional home inspector to assess the property's condition and identify any issues or repairs needed.

7. Make an Offer: Work with your real estate agent to prepare and submit a competitive offer on the property. Consider factors such as market conditions, comparable sales, and the seller's motivations when determining your offer price. Negotiate terms and contingencies to protect your interests.

8. Secure Financing: If your offer is accepted, finalize your mortgage financing. Submit all required documentation to your lender and complete the underwriting process. Obtain a loan commitment letter and review the terms and conditions of your mortgage. This process should be completed first before you start your house hunting because the bank will only approve you for a specific max amount.

9. Close the Deal: Schedule a closing date with the seller and prepare for the closing process. Review all closing documents carefully, including the purchase agreement, loan documents, and settlement statement. Sign the necessary paperwork, pay closing costs and fees, and officially take ownership of the property.

10. Move In, rent it out, and Enjoy: After closing, collect the keys to your new single-family property and celebrate your homeownership. Arrange for any necessary repairs or renovations, move into your new home, and start making memories in your new space or hire a management company to rent out your new home.

What are the types of Real Estate:

Real estate properties come in various types, each with its unique characteristics and investment potential. Here's an overview of different types of real estate properties and typical down payment percentages:

1. Single-Family Homes:

- Stand-alone residential properties designed to house one family.
- Down Payment Percentage: Typically, down payments range from 3% to 20% of the purchase price. The exact percentage depends on factors such as the borrower's credit score, loan program, and lender requirements.

2. Multi-Family Homes (Duplexes, Triplexes, Quadplexes):

- Residential properties containing two or more separate housing units.
- Down Payment Percentage: Down payments usually range from 15% to 25% of the purchase price. Investors may be required to put down a higher percentage compared to single-family homes.

3. Condominiums (Condos):

- Individual units within a larger residential complex, where owners own the unit's interior space and shared common areas.
- Down Payment Percentage: Down payments typically range from 3% to 20% of the purchase price, similar to single-family homes. However, some lenders may require higher down payments due to factors such as condominium association dues and insurance.

4. Townhouses:

- Attached residential properties with multiple floors, usually sharing one or more walls with neighboring units.
- Down Payment Percentage: Down payments are like those for single-family homes, ranging from 3% to 20% of the purchase price.

5. Commercial Properties (Office Buildings, Retail Spaces, Industrial Warehouses):

- Properties used for business purposes, such as offices, retail stores, or manufacturing facilities.
- Down Payment Percentage: Down payments for commercial properties typically range from 15% to 35% of the purchase price. Lenders may require larger down payments due to the higher risks associated with commercial real estate.

6. Vacation Homes:

- Secondary properties used for recreational purposes or as vacation rentals.
- Down Payment Percentage: Down payments for vacation homes are similar to those for primary residences, ranging from 10% to 20% of the purchase price. However, lenders may impose stricter requirements for vacation home financing.

7. Land:

- Description: Undeveloped parcels of land or lots that may be used for future construction or investment purposes.
- Down Payment Percentage: Down payments for land purchases can vary widely, ranging from 20% to 50% or more of the purchase price. Lenders typically require larger down payments for land due to the higher risks and lack of existing structures.

These down payment percentages are general guidelines and may vary based on factors such as the borrower's creditworthiness, loan program, and lender requirements. It's essential to consult with a qualified real estate professional or lender to determine the specific down payment requirements for your desired property type and financing scenario.

The Search for Properties:

For new real estate investors, searching for properties requires careful consideration and research to find suitable investment opportunities. Remember, millionaires use these tactics to increase their wealth and build large real estate portfolios that generate massive amounts of residual income.

Single Family Homes:

1. **Define Investment Criteria:** Begin by defining your investment goals and criteria. Determine factors such as the type of property you're interested in (single-family homes), preferred location, budget, expected return on investment (ROI), and risk tolerance.

ROI (Return On Investment)

To calculate the Return on Investment (ROI) for a single-family home worth $100,000, you need to consider both the initial investment and the potential returns from the property. Here's how to calculate ROI:

Initial Investment:

Determine the total cost of acquiring the property, including the purchase price, closing costs, and any renovation or repair expenses. For example, if the purchase price of the home is $100,000 and closing costs amount to $5,000, the total initial investment would be $105,000.

Potential Returns:

- Estimate the annual rental income you expect to generate from the property. Research similar rental properties in the area to determine a realistic rental rate.

- Calculate the annual rental income by multiplying the monthly rental income by 12.

- For instance, if you anticipate renting the property for $1,000 per month, the annual rental income would be $12,000.

Calculate Operating Expenses:

- Identify the annual expenses associated with owning and maintaining the property, including property taxes, insurance, property management fees, maintenance, repairs, vacancies, and any mortgage payments if applicable.

- Subtract the total annual expenses from the annual rental income to determine the net operating income (NOI).

Calculate ROI:

- Divide the NOI by the initial investment and multiply by 100 to express the ROI as a percentage.

- The formula for calculating ROI is: ROI = (Net Operating Income / Initial Investment) x 100.

For example:

- Annual Rental Income: $12,000
- Annual Expenses (property taxes, insurance, maintenance, etc.): $3,000
- Net Operating Income (NOI): $12,000 - $3,000 = $9,000
- Initial Investment: $105,000

- ROI = ($9,000 / $105,000) x 100 ≈ 8.57%

In this example, the ROI for the single-family home is approximately 8.57%. This indicates that for every dollar invested in the property, you can expect to earn an annual return of 8.57%.

2. Research Local Markets: Conduct thorough research on local real estate markets to identify areas with strong investment potential. Look for neighborhoods experiencing population growth, job opportunities, infrastructure development, and amenities that attract tenants or buyers. Analyze market trends, property values, rental rates, vacancy rates, and other relevant data to assess market viability.

3. Network with Real Estate Professionals: Build relationships with real estate agents, brokers, property managers, and other industry professionals who can provide valuable insights and assistance in your property search. Attend local real estate networking events, join investor groups or forums, and leverage social media platforms to connect with professionals and fellow investors.

4. Utilize Online Resources: Explore online real estate listing platforms, such as Zillow, Realtor.com, Redfin, and Trulia, to search for available properties in your target area. Use filters to narrow down search results based on property type, price range, location, and other criteria. Consider setting up alerts or notifications to receive updates on new listings that meet your preferences.

5. Drive or Walk Around Neighborhoods: Take the time to explore potential investment neighborhoods in person. Drive or walk around different areas to get a feel for the community, observe property conditions, and identify opportunities that may not be listed online. Look for "For Sale" signs, distressed properties, or homes in need of renovation that could offer investment potential.

6. Consider Starting in Your Own Hometown: Starting your real estate investing journey in your own hometown can offer several advantages, such as familiarity with the local market, easier access to properties, and the ability to oversee investments more closely. However, be open to exploring opportunities in nearby or neighboring areas if your hometown lacks viable investment options or if other markets offer better prospects for growth and returns.

7. Evaluate Potential Properties: Once you identify potential properties, conduct thorough due diligence to assess their investment viability. Evaluate factors such as property condition, rental income potential, expenses, cash flow projections, financing options, and potential risks. Consider consulting with a real estate agent, appraiser, or property inspector to obtain professional assessments and insights.

8. Stay Patient and Persistent: Real estate investing requires patience and persistence. It may take time to find the right property that aligns with your investment goals and criteria. Stay proactive in your property search, continue networking, and be prepared to act swiftly when opportunities arise. Remember that finding the perfect investment property is a process, and persistence pays off in the long run.

Types of Real Estate Income Streams:

Real estate investing offers various types of income streams, each providing investors with different financial benefits. Some common types of income associated with real estate investing include:

1. Rental Income: Rental income is generated from tenants who occupy the investor's property and pay rent. This income stream is often considered one of the most significant benefits of real estate investing, as it provides regular, recurring cash flow to property owners. Rental income can help cover property expenses, such as mortgage payments, property taxes, insurance, maintenance costs, and property management fees. Investors can set rental rates based on market conditions, property location, amenities, and other factors.

2. Residual Income: Residual income, also known as passive income, refers to the ongoing revenue generated from real estate investments with minimal ongoing effort or active involvement from the investor. Rental properties are a common source of residual income, as investors receive regular rental payments from tenants without needing to actively work for each dollar earned. Residual income allows investors to build wealth over time and achieve financial freedom by generating income while they sleep.

3. Appreciation: Property appreciation occurs when the value of a real estate asset increases over time due to factors such as market demand, economic growth, inflation, and property improvements. Appreciation can provide investors with significant capital gains when they sell the property for a higher price than they initially paid for it. While appreciation is not guaranteed and may vary depending on market conditions, location, and other factors, it can be a valuable source of wealth accumulation for long-term real estate investors.

4. Equity Build-Up: Equity build-up occurs as the property's mortgage balance decreases over time through regular mortgage payments. With each mortgage payment, a portion goes toward paying down the loan principal, thereby increasing the investor's equity stake in the property. Equity build-up represents the difference between the property's market value and the outstanding mortgage debt. As equity accumulates, investors can leverage it to finance additional real estate investments, access capital for other investment opportunities, or improve their overall financial position.

5. Tax Benefits: Real estate investing offers various tax advantages and deductions that can help investors minimize their tax liability and maximize their after-tax returns. Common tax benefits associated with real estate investing include depreciation deductions, mortgage interest deductions, property tax deductions, operating expenses deductions, and capital gains tax deferral through 1031 exchanges. These tax incentives can significantly enhance the overall profitability of real estate investments and improve investors' cash flow.

6. Cash Flow from Flipping Properties: Flipping properties involves purchasing distressed or undervalued properties, renovating, or improving them, and then selling them for a profit. While flipping properties requires active involvement and carries higher risks compared to rental properties, successful flips can generate substantial short-term profits for investors. Investors can earn cash flow from flipping properties by buying low, adding value through renovations or upgrades, and selling high in a relatively short period.

Real estate investing offers a diverse range of income opportunities, allowing investors to tailor their investment strategies to their financial goals, risk tolerance, and preferred investment approach. By understanding the various income streams associated with real estate investing, investors can make informed decisions to maximize their returns and build long-term wealth through real estate.

To determine how much a first-time buyer would need to purchase a $150,000 home with an interest rate of 5%, we need to consider several factors, including the down payment, closing costs, and other associated expenses. Here's an example breakdown:

1. Down Payment: Typically, first-time homebuyers aim for a down payment between 3% and 20% of the home's purchase price. Let's assume the buyer opts for a 10% down payment on the $150,000 home.

Down Payment = 10% of $150,000

$$= 0.10 \times \$150,000$$

$$= \$15,000$$

2. Loan Amount: The loan amount is the difference between the purchase price of the home and the down payment. In this case:

Loan Amount = Purchase Price - Down Payment

$$= \$150,000 - \$15,000$$

$$= \$135,000$$

3. Interest Rate: Given that the interest rate is 5%, we can calculate the monthly mortgage payment using a standard mortgage calculator or formula.

4. Monthly Mortgage Payment: Using the loan amount and interest rate, we can calculate the monthly mortgage payment using the formula for a fixed-rate mortgage:

Monthly Mortgage Payment = [Loan Amount × (Interest Rate / 12)] / [1 - (1 + Interest Rate / 12)^(-Loan Term in Months)]

Let's assume a typical loan term of 30 years (360 months) for this calculation.

5. Closing Costs: Closing costs typically range from 2% to 5% of the home's purchase price. For this example, let's estimate closing costs at 3% of the purchase price.

Closing Costs = 3% of $150,000

$$= 0.03 \times \$150,000$$

$$= \$4,500$$

6. Total Funds Needed: To determine the total funds needed to purchase the home, we add the down payment and closing costs.

Total Funds Needed = Down Payment + Closing Costs

$$= \$15,000 + \$4,500$$

$$= \$19,500$$

Therefore, a first-time buyer would need approximately $19,500 to purchase a $150,000 home with a 10% down payment and an interest rate of 5%. It's important to note that this is a simplified example, and actual costs may vary based on factors such as the buyer's credit score, lender requirements, property taxes, insurance, and other fees. Additionally, buyers should consult with a mortgage lender or financial advisor to assess their specific financial situation and explore available financing options.

Here's one more example:

To calculate the cost of buying the home, we need to consider the down payment and the loan amount, as well as any additional closing costs. Let's assume the buyer decides to make a down payment of 20%, which is a common requirement for investment properties. Let's use a property purchase cost of $75,000.

First, we calculate the down payment:

Down Payment = Purchase Price × Down Payment Percentage

Down Payment = $75,000 × 0.20

Down Payment = $15,000

Next, we calculate the loan amount:

Loan Amount = Purchase Price - Down Payment

Loan Amount = $75,000 - $15,000

Loan Amount = $60,000

Now, we can calculate the monthly mortgage payment using the loan amount and the interest rate. We'll assume a 30-year fixed-rate mortgage for this calculation:

Using a mortgage calculator or formula, the monthly mortgage payment can be calculated using the loan amount ($60,000), interest rate (5.5% or 0.055), and loan term (30 years or 360 months).

Using the formula for a fixed-rate mortgage:

$M = P[r(1+r)^n]/[(1+r)^n - 1]$

Where:

M = monthly mortgage payment

P = principal loan amount ($60,000)

r = monthly interest rate (annual interest rate divided by 12) = 0.055/12

n = number of payments (loan term in months) = 30 years × 12 months/year = 360 months

Plugging in the values:

r = 0.055/12 = 0.004583

n = 360

M = $60,000[0.004583(1+0.004583)^360] / [(1+0.004583)^360 - 1]

After calculating, we find the monthly mortgage payment to be approximately $339.74.

So, the buyer would need to budget for the down payment of $15,000, plus any closing costs, as well as the monthly mortgage payment of approximately $339.74. Additionally, the buyer should budget for property taxes, insurance, maintenance costs, and potential vacancies when determining the overall cost of purchasing and owning the rental property. Depending on the area and size of the home, this property could be rented out for $1000 or more. This would net you $300-$400 dollars in steady income each month minus your payment, taxes, and insurance.

Types of Programs to Consider when buying a home

There are several types of programs available to aid people in buying properties, particularly for first-time homebuyers. Some of the most common programs include:

1. FHA Loans (Federal Housing Administration): FHA loans are popular among first-time buyers because they typically need lower down payments (as low as 3.5% of the purchase price) and have more flexible credit requirements compared to conventional loans. These loans are insured by the FHA, which allows lenders to offer them with favorable terms.

2. VA Loans (Department of Veterans Affairs): VA loans are available to eligible veterans, active-duty service members, and certain surviving spouses. These loans offer 100% financing (no down payment required) and generally have lower interest rates compared to conventional loans. They are guaranteed by the VA, making them an attractive choice for military personnel and their families.

3. USDA Loans (U.S. Department of Agriculture): USDA loans, also known as Rural Development loans, are designed to help low-to-moderate-income individuals purchase homes in eligible rural areas. These loans offer 100% financing and may have lower interest rates than conventional loans. Eligibility is based on income and the property's location.

4. Conventional Loans: Conventional loans are not insured or guaranteed by the government. They typically require higher credit scores and larger down payments compared to FHA, VA, or USDA loans. However, borrowers with strong credit and financial profiles may qualify for competitive interest rates and terms.

5. Down Payment Assistance Programs (DPA): Many states, cities, and local organizations offer down payment assistance programs to help buyers cover their down payment and closing costs. These programs may provide grants, low-interest loans, or forgivable loans to eligible buyers, particularly those with low to moderate incomes or buying homes in designated areas.

6. First-Time Homebuyer Programs: Some states and municipalities offer specific programs or incentives for first-time homebuyers, such as tax credits, reduced interest rates, or homebuyer education courses. These programs aim to support individuals purchasing their first homes and may provide financial aid or other resources to help them navigate the homebuying process.

These are just a few examples of the programs available to assist you in buying properties. It's essential for prospective buyers to research and explore all available options, as eligibility criteria, terms, and benefits may vary depending on the program and the buyer's individual circumstances. Working with a knowledgeable lender or housing counselor can also help buyers decide the best program for their needs and financial situation.

Other Types of Real Estate Mentioned Previously:

1. Single Family Homes (single families)

2. Multi-Family Homes (Duplexes, Triplexes, Quadplexes):

3. Condominiums (Condos):

4. Townhouses:

5. Commercial Properties (Office Buildings, Retail Spaces, Industrial Warehouses):

6. Vacation Homes:

7. Land:

In conclusion, each of the real estate properties holds the potential to generate substantial income if invested in properly.

- Multi-family homes, such as duplexes, triplexes, and quadplexes, offer the opportunity to earn rental income from multiple units within a single property, maximizing cash flow.

- Condominiums offer a convenient option for investors seeking to own property with shared amenities while benefiting from rental income or potential appreciation.

- Townhouses offer a blend of the privacy of single-family homes and the convenience of shared amenities, making them attractive investment options.

- Commercial properties, including office buildings, retail spaces, and industrial warehouses, can yield significant returns through lease agreements with businesses.

- Vacation homes present an opportunity for both rental income and personal enjoyment, particularly in desirable tourist destinations.

- Lastly, investing in land offers the potential for long-term appreciation or development opportunities, making it a versatile asset class for investors with strategic vision. By carefully evaluating each property type and implementing sound investment strategies, investors can unlock the full income-generating potential of real estate.

Chapter 9: Building Multiple Streams of Income

During a momentous encounter with Mr. Reid, affectionately known as Unc, Michael shared the story of his reunion with Terry during his training trip away. As Michael recounted Terry's insights on investing, Unc responded with his trademark enthusiasm, exclaiming, "Yesssirrr, that's a good thing." Michael always found himself drawn to Unc's words of wisdom, which resonated deeply with him.

Unc, a retired military veteran collecting both retirement and disability checks, along with substantial earnings from his work in Iraq, served as a beacon of inspiration for Michael. With each conversation, Unc shared his ambitious financial goals, aiming to reach $700,000 in the near future and ultimately striving for a million-dollar milestone before leaving Iraq.

Michael was awestruck by Unc's ability to generate and save such significant sums of money. However, he also felt a sense of longing, realizing that he lacked the safety nets of retirement and disability checks. Determined to forge his own path to financial success, Michael contemplated ways to create multiple streams of income, envisioning a future where he too could enjoy the security of multiple checks arriving each month. Inspired by Unc's resilience and determination, Michael embarked on a journey to build his own financial empire, fueled by the pursuit of financial freedom and stability.

Diversifying income sources is not just a smart financial move; it's a crucial strategy for ensuring long-term financial stability. Relying solely on a single source of income leaves individuals vulnerable to unexpected changes, such as job loss or economic downturns. By diversifying their income streams, individuals can spread their risk and create a more resilient financial foundation.

One of the key benefits of diversification is the ability to mitigate risk. When income is derived from multiple sources, a setback in one area is less likely to have a catastrophic impact on overall financial health. For example, if one source of income experiences a decline, other streams can help offset the loss, providing a valuable safety net during challenging times.

Additionally, diversifying income sources can lead to increased opportunities for growth and wealth accumulation. Different income streams may offer varying levels of profitability and growth potential. By tapping into multiple avenues, individuals can maximize their earning potential and accelerate their journey toward financial independence.

Moreover, diversification fosters adaptability and resilience in the face of changing economic conditions. Industries evolve, job markets fluctuate, and unforeseen circumstances arise. Having diverse income streams allows individuals to pivot more easily in response to shifting trends and challenges, ensuring they remain financially secure and adaptable in any environment.

Furthermore, diversifying income sources can provide greater financial freedom and flexibility. Instead of being beholden to a single employer or client, individuals with multiple streams of income have more control over their financial destiny. They can pursue opportunities that align with their passions and interests, knowing that they have built a robust financial foundation to support them.

In summary, diversifying income sources is a fundamental principle of sound financial planning. By spreading risk, increasing opportunities for growth, enhancing adaptability, and providing greater freedom, diversification lays the groundwork for long-term financial stability and success.

Here are ten top ways to create multiple streams of income:

I. Start a Side Business: Launch a side business based on your skills, hobbies, or interests. This could include freelancing, consulting, e-commerce, or offering a specialized service.

2. Invest in Real Estate: Invest in rental properties to generate passive income through rental payments. You can also explore real estate crowdfunding platforms or invest in real estate investment trusts (REITs) for diversification.

3. Dividend Investing: Invest in dividend-paying stocks or dividend-focused mutual funds and ETFs. Dividend income provides a steady stream of passive income, allowing you to benefit from company profits.

4. Create Digital Products: Develop and sell digital products such as e-books, online courses, templates, stock photography, or software applications. Once created, digital products can generate passive income with minimal ongoing effort.

5. Affiliate Marketing: Partner with companies to promote their products or services and earn a commission for each sale or referral you generate. Affiliate marketing can be done through blogs, social media, or niche websites.

6. Peer-to-Peer Lending: Invest in peer-to-peer lending platforms where you can lend money to individuals or businesses in exchange for interest payments. Platforms like Prosper and Lending Club offer opportunities for passive income generation.

7. Create a YouTube Channel or Podcast: Build a following on YouTube or start a podcast on a topic you're passionate about. Once you have a sizable audience, you can monetize your content through advertising, sponsorships, and merchandise sales.

8. Offer Online Courses or Coaching: Share your expertise by creating and selling online courses, workshops, or coaching sessions. Platforms like Udemy, Teachable, and Coach.me provide tools to monetize your knowledge and skills.

9. Rental Income from Assets: Rent out assets such as vehicles, equipment, or storage space to generate rental income. This could include renting out a spare room on Airbnb or leasing out your car when you're not using it.

10. Royalties and Licensing: Create intellectual property such as music, books, or inventions and license them for royalties. Royalties can provide passive income over time as your creations are used or sold.

By diversifying your income streams across different sources, you can reduce reliance on any single source of income and build a more resilient financial portfolio. Consider your skills, interests, and risk tolerance when exploring these opportunities and aim to create a balanced mix of active and passive income streams.

Passive income opportunities provide a pathway to financial freedom by allowing individuals to generate income with minimal ongoing effort. Among the most popular passive income streams are rental properties, dividend stocks, and online businesses.

Rental properties offer a reliable source of passive income through rental payments from tenants. By investing in residential or commercial real estate, individuals can earn consistent cash flow while also benefiting from potential property appreciation over time. Rental properties provide a hands-off income stream for investors who choose to outsource property management responsibilities.

Dividend stocks are another attractive option for passive income seekers. When investors purchase shares of dividend-paying companies, they receive regular dividend payments as a reward for their investment. Dividend stocks offer a source of passive income that can be reinvested to compound wealth over time or used to cover living expenses.

Online businesses present lucrative opportunities for generating passive income through various digital channels. From e-commerce stores and affiliate marketing to digital products and online courses, individuals can leverage the power of the internet to create scalable income streams. Once established, online businesses can generate passive income through automated sales, digital product downloads, and recurring subscription fees.

By diversifying across rental properties, dividend stocks, and online businesses, individuals can build a robust portfolio of passive income streams. Each opportunity offers unique advantages and considerations, allowing investors to tailor their passive income strategy to their financial goals and risk tolerance. With careful planning and prudent investment decisions, passive income can provide financial stability and long-term wealth accumulation.

Little did Michael know, he had inadvertently stumbled upon a second stream of income by renting out his primary home. As he delved deeper into the world of real estate investing, Michael realized the potential for expanding his portfolio by buying additional rental properties. Inspired by his newfound knowledge and driven by his financial goals, Michael set out to buy one new property each year.

During a visit back home to see his family, Michael serendipitously encountered an opportunity that would change the trajectory of his investment journey. While cruising through the neighborhood where his primary property was located, Michael spotted a familiar house for sale. Having frequented the home and acquainted himself with its previous owners, Michael immediately recognized the potential of the property.

Without hesitation, Michael reached out to his trusted real estate agent to inquire about the home's status. To his surprise, he learned that the house had been foreclosed upon and was listed for sale at a remarkably low price of $56,000. Recognizing the incredible value proposition, Michael wasted no time in contacting his bank to secure a pre-approval for the asking price.

With no competing offers in sight, Michael's swift action paid off as his offer was swiftly accepted by the sellers. Once again, Michael found himself in the right place at the right time, seizing an opportunity to expand his investment income and further solidify his financial future.

A Millionaires Mindset:

A millionaire's mindset on multiple streams of income is rooted in the understanding that true wealth and financial freedom are achieved not solely through hard work but through strategic planning and diversification of income sources. Instead of relying on a single source of income, millionaires recognize the importance of cultivating multiple streams that generate revenue consistently.

By establishing multiple streams of income, millionaires create a safety net that cushions them against economic downturns or job loss. This diversified approach ensures that they are not overly reliant on any single source of revenue, thereby reducing financial vulnerability.

Moreover, having multiple streams of income allows millionaires to enjoy greater flexibility and autonomy in their lives. Rather than being tied to a traditional nine-to-five job, they have the freedom to pursue their passions, explore new opportunities, and spend time with loved ones.

Furthermore, millionaires understand the power of passive income—the kind of income that continues to flow in even when they're not actively working. Whether it's through rental properties, dividend-paying stocks, royalties from intellectual property, or income generated from online businesses, passive income provides a steady stream of cash flow that requires minimal ongoing effort.

In addition to generating income, millionaires also prioritize saving and investing their earnings wisely. Instead of succumbing to lifestyle inflation, where expenses rise in tandem with income, they adopt a frugal mindset and prioritize saving a significant portion of their earnings.

By consistently saving and investing their multiple streams of income, millionaires are able to accelerate wealth accumulation and build long-term financial security. They understand that wealth is not just about earning a high income but about effectively managing and growing the resources they have.

In essence, the millionaire's mindset is characterized by a proactive approach to financial management, a commitment to diversification, and a focus on building wealth through smart saving, investing, and strategic income generation. Through these principles, they create a solid foundation for long-term prosperity and abundance.

With the addition of the second home to Michael's investment portfolio, along with his ongoing endeavors in the stock market and the steady income from his job, Michael found himself gradually transitioning his ordinary thinking mind into a millionaire mindset. While he started as an ordinary individual, the combination of his various income streams was subtly shaping him into an extraordinary individual, even without him fully realizing it.

The acquisition of the second property marked another milestone in Michael's journey towards financial independence and wealth accumulation. It demonstrated his proactive approach to investing and his willingness to seize opportunities when they arose. By diversifying his investments beyond the stock market and into real estate, Michael was taking deliberate steps to build a robust financial foundation that could withstand economic fluctuations and provide long-term stability.

Simultaneously, Michael's involvement in the stock market continued to sharpen his understanding of investment strategies and financial markets. While he encountered both successes and setbacks along the way, each experience served as a valuable lesson in risk management, patience, and resilience. Over time, Michael became increasingly adept at navigating the complexities of stock trading and perfecting his investment decisions to maximize returns.

Additionally, the steady income from his job provided Michael with a sense of security and stability, allowing him to pursue his investment ventures with confidence. While his job served as a reliable source of income, it also fueled his ambition to achieve greater financial success and freedom.

As Michael reflected on his evolving financial journey, he realized that he was gradually aligning his mindset with that of a millionaire. He began to prioritize wealth-building strategies, such as saving, investing, and expanding his income streams, with a long-term perspective in mind. While he may have started as an ordinary guy, Michael's determination and forward-thinking mindset were propelling him towards extraordinary achievements in the realm of finance and beyond.

Rental Income Stream

Rental income streams can serve as powerful vehicles for propelling individuals towards their financial goals in several ways. Firstly, rental properties offer a consistent source of passive income, providing a steady stream of cash flow each month. This income can be used to cover expenses, such as mortgage payments, property maintenance, and taxes, while still leaving surplus funds for savings and investments.

Moreover, rental properties have the potential to appreciate in value over time, leading to equity buildup for the property owner. As property values increase, so does the owner's net worth, allowing them to leverage their assets for further investments or financial endeavors.

Additionally, rental income streams offer diversification within an investment portfolio, reducing reliance on traditional investment vehicles such as stocks and bonds. This diversification can help mitigate risk and provide stability during economic downturns or market fluctuations.

To make the most of rental income streams and accelerate financial growth, individuals can consider reinvesting their earnings into various wealth-building strategies. One approach is to reinvest rental profits into buying additional rental properties, thereby expanding their real estate portfolio, and increasing overall rental income.

Furthermore, individuals can allocate a portion of their rental income towards paying down existing mortgages or financing new real estate acquisitions. By reducing debt and leveraging financing wisely, investors can optimize their returns and enhance cash flow over the long term.

Another strategy is to diversify investments by allocating rental income towards other asset classes, such as stocks, bonds, or mutual funds. This approach can help individuals build a well-rounded investment portfolio that generates multiple streams of income and hedges against market volatility.

Moreover, individuals can reinvest rental income into property improvements or renovations, increasing the value and desirability of their rental properties. Upgrading amenities, enhancing curb appeal, or implementing energy-efficient upgrades can attract higher-quality tenants and command higher rental rates, thereby boosting overall rental income.

Ultimately, the key to leveraging rental income streams for financial growth lies in prudent financial management, strategic reinvestment, and a long-term investment mindset. By maximizing the potential of rental properties and diversifying income sources, individuals can accelerate their journey towards achieving their financial goals and building wealth for the future.

Here's How to leverage one property to buy another:

Taking equity from one rental property to buy another is a common strategy known as leveraging equity. Here's how it typically works:

1. Build Equity: Equity in a rental property is built over time as the property's value increases and the mortgage balance decreases through mortgage payments. Additionally, any improvements made to the property can also contribute to increased equity.

2. Obtain a Home Equity Loan or Line of Credit: Once a significant amount of equity has been built in a rental property, the property owner can apply for a home equity loan or a home equity line of credit (HELOC). These financial products allow property owners to borrow against the equity in their property.

3. Use Equity as Down Payment: The proceeds from the home equity loan or HELOC can then be used as a down payment on another rental property. This allows the property owner to leverage the equity in their existing property to acquire additional real estate assets.

4. Purchase Another Property: With the funds from the home equity loan or HELOC, the property owner can purchase another rental property. This new property can then be used to generate rental income, further diversifying the owner's real estate portfolio, and potentially increasing overall cash flow.

5. Manage Cash Flow: It's important to carefully consider the cash flow implications of taking equity from one property to buy another. Property owners should assess whether the rental income from the new property, combined with any existing rental income, will be sufficient to cover expenses such as mortgage payments, property taxes, insurance, and maintenance costs.

6. Evaluate Risks: While leveraging equity can be a powerful strategy for expanding a real estate portfolio, it also involves risks. Property values may fluctuate, interest rates may change, and rental markets can be unpredictable. Property owners should conduct thorough due diligence and consider potential risks before using equity to purchase additional properties.

Overall, leveraging equity from one rental property to buy another can be an effective way to grow a real estate portfolio and increase long-term wealth accumulation. However, it's essential to approach this strategy prudently and seek professional advice when necessary to mitigate risks and maximize potential returns.

Investing Streams of Income:

401(k) accounts and stock investing can indeed play significant roles in creating income streams that propel individuals towards their financial goals. Here's how they can do so:

I. **401(k) Accounts:** These employer-sponsored retirement accounts offer individuals the opportunity to save for retirement through pre-tax contributions, often with employer matching contributions. Over time, contributions to a 401(k) can grow tax-deferred, allowing for potential compound growth. Upon retirement, individuals can withdraw funds from their 401(k) to supplement their income.

2. **Stock Investing:** Investing in individual stocks or exchange-traded funds (ETFs) can provide another avenue for generating income. Dividend-paying stocks, in particular, can offer regular cash payments to investors. Additionally, stock investments have the potential for capital appreciation, meaning the value of the investment can increase over time.

To maximize the growth of these income streams, individuals can consider the following strategies:

I. **Reinvest Dividends:** Instead of cashing out dividends received from stocks, reinvest them back into the investment account. This allows for compound growth, as dividends are used to purchase additional shares, which can then generate more dividends in the future.

2. **Dollar-Cost Averaging:** Rather than trying to time the market, employ a dollar-cost averaging strategy by consistently investing a fixed amount of money into stocks or ETFs at regular intervals. This approach helps smooth out the impact of market volatility and can lead to better long-term returns.

3. **Regular Portfolio Review:** Periodically review and rebalance your investment portfolio to ensure it aligns with your financial goals and risk tolerance. Adjust asset allocations as needed to maintain a diversified portfolio that can weather various market conditions.

4. Consider Tax-Efficient Strategies: Be mindful of tax implications when managing your investment portfolio. Utilize tax-advantaged accounts such as IRAs and Roth IRAs to minimize taxes on investment gains. Additionally, tax-loss harvesting can be employed to offset capital gains with capital losses, reducing overall tax liabilities.

5. Explore Additional Investment Opportunities: Diversify your investment portfolio by exploring alternative investment opportunities such as real estate, bonds, or commodities. This can help spread risk and potentially enhance overall returns.

By implementing these strategies, individuals can harness the power of 401(k) accounts and stock investing to create robust income streams that contribute to their financial security and help them achieve their long-term goals.

Day trading and Option trading Streams of Income:

Day trading and option trading can indeed be lucrative streams of income if approached with discipline, strategy, and risk management. Here's how these activities can serve as income streams when done correctly:

1. Active Trading Strategy: Day trading involves buying and selling financial instruments within the same trading day, aiming to capitalize on short-term price movements. Option trading involves buying and selling options contracts, which grant the holder the right to buy or sell an underlying asset at a specified price within a set timeframe. Both strategies require active monitoring of the market and making quick decisions based on technical and fundamental analysis.

2. Profit Generation: Successful day traders and option traders can generate profits by accurately predicting short-term price movements or taking advantage of volatility in the market. By buying low and selling high (or vice versa) within a single trading session, day traders can profit from price fluctuations. Similarly, option traders can profit from changes in the price of the underlying asset or changes in implied volatility.

3. Risk Management: Effective risk management is crucial when engaging in day trading and option trading. Traders must set clear entry and exit points, establish stop-loss orders to limit potential losses, and avoid overleveraging their positions. Diversification of trading strategies and assets can also help mitigate risk.

4. Taking Profits: Day traders and option traders often follow the principle of taking profits when targets are met or when the market conditions indicate a favorable opportunity. This may involve selling a portion of their positions to lock in gains while allowing the remainder to continue running if the market trends favorably.

5. Reinvestment: Reinvesting profits from successful trades can help compound returns over time. Day traders and option traders may allocate a portion of their profits to reinvest in new trades or to build a diversified investment portfolio across various asset classes. This approach can help grow their capital and potentially increase their overall income over the long term.

6. Continuous Learning: Day trading and option trading require ongoing education and skill development. Successful traders stay informed about market trends, technical analysis tools, and trading strategies. They continuously refine their approaches based on their experiences and adapt to changes in market conditions.

While day trading and option trading offer the potential for significant returns, they also carry inherent risks, including the risk of substantial losses. As such, individuals considering these activities should thoroughly educate themselves, start with small investments, and be prepared to accept the possibility of losses. Additionally, seeking guidance from experienced traders or financial advisors can provide valuable insights and help mitigate risks.

Laying a solid financial foundation is crucial for anyone looking to embark on the journey of creating multiple streams of income. It's akin to building a sturdy structure upon which you can construct your wealth-building endeavors.

First and foremost, paying off debt is key. Debt can weigh heavily on your finances, draining your resources and limiting your ability to invest in income-generating assets. By eliminating high-interest debt and managing your finances responsibly, you free up valuable resources that can be redirected towards wealth-building activities.

Budgeting and saving are equally important components of this foundation. A well-crafted budget allows you to track your expenses, identify areas where you can cut back, and allocate funds towards your financial goals. Saving regularly ensures that you have a financial cushion to fall back on in case of emergencies and provides capital for investment opportunities.

Once you have your financial house in order, you're in a much stronger position to take action on creating multiple streams of income. Whether it's investing in real estate, starting a side hustle, or venturing into the stock market, having a solid foundation gives you the confidence and resources to pursue these opportunities with conviction.

Moreover, the discipline and financial literacy gained from paying off debt, budgeting, and saving are invaluable assets as you navigate the complexities of generating additional income. They instill good habits, such as living within your means, managing risk, and making informed financial decisions, which are essential for long-term success.

In essence, laying a solid foundation through debt repayment, budgeting, and saving sets the stage for financial freedom and opens up a world of possibilities for creating multiple streams of income. It's the first step towards building wealth and achieving your financial goals, allowing you to seize opportunities and thrive in today's dynamic economic landscape.

Now that you've learned about the various ways to create multiple streams of income and have seen how Michael seized an opportunity to purchase his second property, it's time for you to embark on your own journey of financial empowerment. While it may seem daunting at first, remember that success often lies just beyond the comfort zone.

By taking inspiration from Michael's story and exploring new avenues for generating income, you too can unlock a world of possibilities. Whether it's through real estate investments, stock trading, starting a side business, or pursuing passive income opportunities, there are countless paths to financial freedom.

Embrace the mindset of continuous learning and adaptation as you navigate the ups and downs of your journey. Stay open to new opportunities and be willing to take calculated risks along the way. Remember, every step forward, no matter how small, brings you closer to your goals.

With determination, perseverance, and a willingness to step outside the box, you have the power to shape your financial destiny. The world is full of opportunities waiting to be seized, and with the right mindset and approach, anything is possible. So go forth with confidence, and start building the life of abundance and prosperity that you deserve.

Chapter 10: The Role of Discipline and Patience

Discipline and patience are the cornerstone virtues that underpin the achievement of financial goals. In chapter 10, we delve deep into the profound significance of these attributes in navigating the complexities of personal finance. At its core, discipline entails the consistent application of self-control and adherence to a predetermined financial plan. It involves making sound decisions even when faced with temptation or adversity. Patience, on the other hand, is the ability to tolerate delay without becoming frustrated or impulsive. Together, these virtues form a powerful duo that can propel individuals towards financial success.

One of the key lessons highlighted in this chapter is the importance of setting clear, achievable goals and staying committed to them over the long term. Without discipline, it's easy to stray off course or succumb to short-term gratification at the expense of long-term prosperity. Patience serves as the guiding force that allows individuals to stay focused on their goals despite inevitable setbacks or market fluctuations. Moreover, discipline and patience go hand in hand when it comes to managing finances responsibly.

This involves cultivating healthy spending habits, saving diligently, and investing wisely. Without discipline, overspending and impulsive financial decisions can derail even the most well-laid plans. Patience is particularly crucial in the realm of investing, where short-term fluctuations are commonplace. It's essential to resist the urge to chase quick gains and instead adopt a patient approach focused on long-term growth. Furthermore, discipline extends to areas such as debt management, where maintaining regular payments and avoiding unnecessary debt are paramount. Patience comes into play here as individuals work towards paying off debts methodically, understanding that it may take time to achieve financial freedom. In essence, discipline and patience serve as the guiding principles that shape one's financial journey.

They instill the resilience needed to weather storms, the determination to stay on course, and the foresight to prioritize long-term stability over short-term gratification. This chapter underscores the notion that financial success is not solely determined by luck or circumstance but rather by the deliberate cultivation of these virtues. It emphasizes the need for consistent effort and a steadfast commitment to one's financial goals. Moreover, discipline and patience are not innate traits but rather skills that can be developed and honed over time.

By cultivating these virtues, individuals empower themselves to take control of their financial futures and build a solid foundation for lasting prosperity. In conclusion, chapter 9 serves as a poignant reminder of the indispensable role that discipline and patience play in achieving financial well-being. It encourages readers to embrace these virtues wholeheartedly and integrate them into every aspect of their financial lives. For it is through discipline and patience that true financial empowerment is attained, allowing individuals to chart a course towards a brighter and more secure future.

Michael's lack of patience was evident in his younger years as he chased after numerous get-rich-quick schemes, none of which yielded the desired results. He was constantly seeking shortcuts to wealth, unwilling to put in the necessary time and effort for sustainable success. These ventures often led to disappointment and financial setbacks, further exacerbating his impatience.

However, it wasn't until Michael shifted his focus away from instant gratification and towards more sustainable practices that his fortunes began to change. It was during a mundane day at the car wash, where Michael was simply going about his daily routine, that opportunity unexpectedly knocked on his door. This encounter served as a wake-up call, prompting Michael to reassess his approach to financial success. Despite the initial excitement, Michael soon found himself in a position where all he could do was wait for his friend Terry to come through for him. This period of waiting tested Michael's patience like never before, forcing him to confront his impulsive tendencies and adopt a more measured approach.

Even when communication with Terry went silent, Michael remained steadfast, refusing to let uncertainty derail his progress. The experience taught him the value of patience and resilience in the face of adversity. When Michael found himself stationed in Iraq with ample time on his hands, he seized the opportunity to educate himself and become financially literate. He recognized that true wealth was built through knowledge and strategic planning, not quick fixes, or shortcuts. Through disciplined study and careful planning, Michael laid the groundwork for his long-term financial freedom.

While he still struggled with impatience in other aspects of his life, Michael understood the importance of playing the long game when it came to his finances. He recognized that time was a powerful ally in building wealth and that patience was the key to unlocking its full potential. By embracing discipline and patience, Michael set himself and his family on a path towards a brighter and more secure future. He understood that financial success wasn't about instant gratification but rather about making deliberate choices and staying the course, even when faced with challenges along the way. In the end, Michael's journey serves as a testament to the transformative power of discipline and patience in achieving lasting prosperity.

Staying focused and resilient in the face of challenges and setbacks is essential for achieving success and personal growth.

Here are some strategies to help you maintain your focus and bounce back stronger:

1. Maintain a Positive Attitude: Cultivate a positive mindset that sees challenges as opportunities for growth rather than insurmountable obstacles.

2. Set Clear Goals: Define specific, achievable goals that give you direction and purpose. Having a clear vision of what you want to achieve helps you stay focused during difficult times.

3. Develop a Routine: Establishing a daily routine can provide structure and stability, making it easier to stay focused and productive, even when facing adversity.

4. Practice Self-Care: Take care of your physical, emotional, and mental well-being by prioritizing activities like exercise, sleep, healthy eating, and relaxation.

5. Stay Flexible: Be willing to adapt and adjust your plans as needed in response to changing circumstances. Flexibility is key to overcoming unexpected challenges.

6. Seek Support: Don't be afraid to reach out to friends, family, mentors, or support groups for encouragement and guidance during tough times.

7. Focus on Solutions: Instead of dwelling on problems, focus on finding solutions and taking proactive steps to address them.

8. Learn from Failure: View setbacks as opportunities to learn and grow. Reflect on what went wrong, identify lessons learned, and use them to improve your approach in the future.

9. Practice Gratitude: Cultivate an attitude of gratitude by focusing on the positive aspects of your life and expressing appreciation for the things you have.

10. Stay Present: Practice mindfulness and stay grounded in the present moment. Worrying about the past or future can distract you from the task at hand.

11. Visualize Success: Take time to visualize yourself overcoming challenges and achieving your goals. This can help you stay motivated and focused on the end result.

12. Break Tasks Down: Break larger tasks or goals into smaller, more manageable steps. This makes them feel less overwhelming and easier to tackle.

13. Stay Committed: Stay committed to your goals and persevere, even when progress seems slow or obstacles arise. Remember why you started and keep pushing forward.

14. Celebrate Small Wins: Acknowledge and celebrate your progress, no matter how small. This boosts your confidence and motivates you to keep going.

15. Stay Inspired: Surround yourself with sources of inspiration, whether it's through books, podcasts, or connecting with like-minded individuals. Drawing inspiration from others can help fuel your own resilience and determination.

16. Limit Distractions: Identify and minimize distractions that pull you away from your goals. This may involve setting boundaries with technology, creating a dedicated workspace, or managing your time more effectively.

17. Stay Educated: Continuously seek opportunities to gain experience and grow, whether through formal education, professional development, or self-directed learning. Knowledge is power, and staying informed can help you navigate challenges more effectively.

18. Practice Patience: Understand that progress takes time and setbacks are a natural part of the journey. Be patient with yourself and trust in the process.

19. Stay Persistent: Persevere in the face of adversity and setbacks. Remember that every setback is an opportunity to learn and grow stronger.

20. Focus on the Long-Term: Keep your long-term goals in mind and remind yourself that setbacks are temporary. Stay focused on the bigger picture and keep moving forward, one step at a time.

Implementing these strategies and staying disciplined and resilient, you can overcome challenges and setbacks on your journey to success. Remember that resilience is a skill that can be developed and strengthened over time, and staying focused is key to achieving your goals.

Top 10 Steps for Staying Focused and Resilient:

• Develop a growth mindset.
• Set realistic expectations.
• Practice self-compassion.
• Focus on what you can control.
• Seek support from others.
• Stay present with mindfulness.
• Break tasks into manageable steps.
• Celebrate progress along the way.
• Learn from setbacks and failures.
• Stay persistent and resilient in pursuit of your goals.

Discipline and patience are essential virtues when it comes to investing in various avenues such as the stock markets, company 401(k) plans, and real estate.

Here's how to apply these principles effectively in each scenario.

Discipline in the Stock Market:

1. Develop a Long-Term Strategy: Create an investment plan that aligns with your financial goals and risk tolerance. Focus on long-term growth rather than short-term fluctuations.

2. Diversify Your Portfolio: Spread your investments across different asset classes and industries to minimize risk. This helps cushion the impact of market volatility.

3. Stay Informed but Avoid Overreacting: Keep yourself updated on market trends and news, but avoid making impulsive decisions based on short-term fluctuations. Stick to your investment strategy and resist the urge to constantly buy and sell.

4. Stick to Your Investment Plan: Maintain discipline by sticking to your predetermined investment plan, even during market downturns. Avoid making emotional decisions based on fear or greed.

5. Regularly Review and Rebalance Your Portfolio: Periodically review your portfolio to ensure it remains aligned with your investment objectives. Rebalance as needed to maintain your desired asset allocation.

Company 401(k) Plans:

1. Maximize Contributions: Take full advantage of your employer's matching contributions, as they represent free money towards your retirement savings.

2. Choose a Suitable Investment Mix: Select investment options within your 401(k) plan that match your risk tolerance and time horizon. Consider factors such as asset allocation, diversification, and fees.

3. Automate Contributions: Set up automatic contributions to your 401(k) to ensure consistent saving and dollar-cost averaging, which can help mitigate market volatility.

4. Monitor Performance Regularly: Keep track of your 401(k) investments' performance but avoid making knee-jerk reactions to short-term fluctuations. Stay focused on your long-term retirement goals.

5. Review Investment Options Annually: Review your investment options within your 401(k) plan annually to ensure they continue to meet your needs and objectives. Make adjustments as necessary.

Real Estate Investing:

1. Do Your Research: Conduct thorough research on the local real estate market, including property values, rental rates, and potential for appreciation.

2. Set Clear Investment Criteria: Define your investment criteria, such as desired property type, location, and expected return on investment (ROI). This helps narrow down your options and stay focused.

3. Stick to Your Budget: Set a realistic budget and stick to it when searching for investment properties. Avoid stretching yourself too thin financially, as this can lead to unnecessary stress and risk.

4. Be Patient in the Buying Process: Take your time when evaluating potential investment properties. Don't rush into a purchase out of fear of missing out. Be disciplined in sticking to your investment criteria.

5. Plan for the Long Term: Realize that real estate investing is a long-term endeavor. Be patient and understand that building wealth through real estate takes time and requires a commitment to managing properties effectively.

Overall, discipline and patience are crucial when investing in the stock markets, company 401(k) plans, and real estate. By staying disciplined in adhering to your investment plan and exercising patience during periods of market volatility or uncertainty, you increase your chances of achieving long-term financial success.

Being disciplined and patient when saving for your emergency fund and financial future is essential for achieving long-term financial stability and security.

Here's how to apply these principles effectively:

1. Set Clear Savings Goals: Define specific, achievable goals for your emergency fund and long-term financial future. Having clear objectives helps you stay focused and motivated to save.

2. Create a Budget: Develop a realistic budget that outlines your income, expenses, and savings goals. Track your spending and identify areas where you can cut back to increase your savings rate.

3. Prioritize Saving: Make saving a priority by treating it as a non-negotiable expense. Set up automatic transfers from your paycheck to your savings account to ensure consistent contributions.

4. Start Small and Increase Over Time: If you're struggling to save, start with small, manageable amounts and gradually increase your savings rate as your income grows or expenses decrease.

5. Build an Emergency Fund: Aim to save three to six months' worth of living expenses in your emergency fund to cover unexpected expenses or financial emergencies. Be patient and prioritize building this fund before focusing on other financial goals.

6. Separate Savings Accounts: Consider opening separate savings accounts for different financial goals, such as emergencies, vacations, or a down payment on a house. This helps you track progress toward each goal and avoid dipping into funds earmarked for emergencies. An online high yield savings account is a great option because it's not as easy to access the money, but it can be ready available with a quick transfer to your primary banking account. An online account also allows you to have a debit card associated with it but I would advise to use the account as a savings mechanism only and if you need the money, transfer it to your bank account.

7. Avoid Impulse Spending: Practice discipline by resisting the temptation to make impulse purchases or splurge on unnecessary items. Before making a purchase, ask yourself if it aligns with your financial goals and priorities.

8. Stay Focused on the Long Term: Keep your long-term financial goals in mind and remind yourself of the importance of staying disciplined and patient, even when faced with short-term temptations or setbacks.

9. Celebrate Milestones: Acknowledge and celebrate your savings milestones along the way, whether it's reaching a certain dollar amount in your emergency fund or achieving a specific savings goal. Celebrating your progress helps reinforce positive financial habits and motivates you to keep going.

10. Review and Adjust Regularly: Periodically review your savings goals and progress to ensure they remain relevant and achievable. Adjust your budget and savings plan as needed based on changes in your financial situation or priorities.

By staying disciplined and patient when saving for your emergency fund and financial future, you can build a solid foundation for long-term financial success. Remember that saving takes time and consistency, but the rewards of financial security and peace of mind are well worth the effort.

In conclusion, Michael's journey is a testament to the power of discipline and patience in achieving financial success. Despite experiencing numerous setbacks and financial losses while chasing get-rich-quick schemes, Michael ultimately learned valuable lessons that transformed his approach to money management. Through perseverance and determination, he realized that true wealth is built steadily over time through disciplined budgeting, debt repayment, saving, and investing. By staying committed to his financial goals and exercising patience,

Michael was able to overcome adversity and create multiple streams of income that set him on the path to long-term financial stability and prosperity. His story serves as an inspiration to others, highlighting the importance of staying disciplined and patient in the pursuit of financial freedom. Through diligence and perseverance, anyone can achieve their financial goals and build a brighter future for themselves and their loved ones.

Chapter 11: Managing Wealth and Risk

Before delving into the intricacies of wealth management and risk mitigation, let's journey back to Michael's story, a narrative that promises to leave a lasting impression on your life and may profoundly shake you to your core.

The End of An Era:

In Chapter 11 of managing wealth and risk, Michael's story unfolds with gripping intensity, revealing the depths of his courage and resilience as he faces a risk like no other during his final days in Iraq. As Michael reached financial freedom, having conquered debts, and excelled in his career as one of the top technical personnel with his company, he embarked on a journey that would test his resolve in ways he never imagined.

It began with a simple phone call, a summons to another site of critical importance managed by another technical expert. The urgency in the caller's voice mirrored the gravity of the situation—the site had been incapacitated for two days, and Michael was the last hope for its revival. Without hesitation, Michael accepted the daunting task, knowing the stakes were high and the risks even higher. Michael consulted with his dear friend and mentor Mr. Reid and received encouraging words to do what was needed. Michael knew there were no flights and was booked on the first moving convoy.

The next morning, as dawn broke over the war-torn landscape of Iraq, Michael prepared for the journey ahead. With no Blackhawk or Chinook Helicopter flights available for two days, Michael thought about the trip ahead and checked for last minute flights for that day but Michael had no choice but to embark on a road convoy—a perilous endeavor fraught with danger at every turn. Despite his trepidation, Michael steeled himself for the journey, his mind racing with thoughts of the task awaiting him at Camp Victory.

As Michael joined his fellow riders and military personnel at the rendezvous point, the air crackled with tension and anticipation. Water and snacks were distributed, a meager offering in the face of the imminent peril that lay ahead. With three vehicles in the convoy, Michael found himself in the lead vehicle, an MRAP (Mine Resistant Ambush Protected) designed to withstand ambushes and explosives—a grim reminder of the dangers lurking in the shadows.

As the convoy pressed forward, Michael's thoughts turned to the task at hand, his mind consumed with plans to rectify the issue at the site. But his moment of reverie was shattered in an instant—a deafening blast reverberated through the air, sending shockwaves of terror through the convoy. In the chaos that ensued, Michael's senses were overwhelmed, his mind struggling to understand the devastation unfolding around him. The blast felt as if it sucked all of the air out of the vehicle and stirred the dust inside the vehicle making it cloudy.

As Michael emerged from the wreckage behind the MRAP, his heart pounded with a mixture of relief and horror. The vehicle behind him, a Humvee carrying three soldiers, lay in ruins, its occupants caught in the merciless grip of fate. The vehicle was unrecognizable and Michael wondered, how could a blast do this to a vehicle of that caliber. Miraculously, only one soldier survived the blast in that vehicle, the gunner. The gunner was atop of the vehicle and the devastation that ripped through the Humvee took his legs. The gunner was in complete shock but was alive as Michael and other soldiers helped pull the soldier to safety. This was a stark reminder of the fragility of life in a war zone.

In the aftermath of the explosion, Michael grappled with the trauma of what he had witnessed, his mind reeling from the magnitude of the disaster. Yet amidst the chaos, he found solace in the courage and resilience of his fellow soldiers, who rallied together to protect and defend one another in the face of overwhelming adversity. After a short period, from the clear blue skies, arrived 2 war fighting Apache Helicopters, sent in to provide eyes in the sky to protect them all at all costs.

As the dust settled and other ground support reinforcements arrived, Michael and his crew were escorted to safety, their bodies intact but their spirits shaken to the core. For Michael, the harrowing ordeal served as a wake-up call—a stark reminder of the risks he faced every day in the line of duty with the soldiers.

In the days that followed, Michael wrestled with the decision that loomed before him—was the risk worth the reward? With his mother's worried face haunting his thoughts, Michael made the difficult choice to end his time in Iraq, unwilling to tempt fate any longer.

As Michael returned home to the embrace of his loved ones, he carried with him the scars of his ordeal, a constant reminder of the sacrifices made in the pursuit of freedom and security. Yet amidst the darkness, there shone a glimmer of hope—a testament to Michael's unwavering courage and resilience in the face of unimaginable adversity. To this day, Michael has never shared these narrow escape stories with his family especially his mother. Michael knew how much his mother worried about him since the day he started this journey. Knowing her only son was this close to never coming home again would worry her to a sickening state. Michael's mother and family will hear this story for the first time through this book as you are   .

In the end, Michael's journey serves as a powerful reminder of the true cost of war—the lives lost, the sacrifices made, and the indomitable spirit of those who dare to dream of a better tomorrow. And as Michael embarks on the next chapter of his life, his story serves as an inspiration to us all—a testament to the power of hope, resilience, and the enduring human spirit. Michael gives credit to the brave soldiers that day and all armed forces that have these experiences each day during war. Now it was time for Michael to move on and prepare for his next phase of life.

Michael extends his deepest gratitude to the exceptional individuals who became his lifelong friends and comrades during his time in Iraq. To Terry, Mr. Reid, Doug, Bull, Gaynel, Eric B, Maria, Derick A, Fred S, Tupou, Brendon R., Tre, Taylor, Speight, Ashley, Phil G, and numerous other civilians and soldiers, your unwavering support and camaraderie have been invaluable on this journey. Additionally, Michael expresses profound appreciation to the courageous soldiers who risked their lives to save him during the harrowing roadside bomb incident. Their heroism and selflessness are eternally remembered, and Michael owes them a debt of gratitude for their extraordinary efforts.

As we conclude Michael's journey in Iraq, it's clear that his story doesn't end here. There are more successes awaiting him in the pages of this book. In life, there are moments when risks become too great, and it becomes imperative to carefully assess them. Michael recalled the words he shared with his mother upon his return home: "If I don't make it, at least I tried." Well, my friends, Michael not only tried but succeeded.

Let's dive in to managing wealth and mitigating risks.

Managing Wealth and Mitigating Risks:

As we explore the multifaceted realm of managing wealth and mitigating risks to ensure its preservation and protection. A cornerstone of this endeavor is the strategic implementation of various strategies aimed at safeguarding wealth and minimizing potential losses. Insurance emerges as a pivotal tool in this pursuit, offering protection against unforeseen events and mitigating financial risks. Health insurance shields individuals from the financial burden of medical expenses, while life insurance provides a safety net for loved ones in the event of the policyholder's death.

Disability insurance offers income protection if a disability that prevents one from working. Property and casualty insurance safeguard assets against damage or loss due to events like fire, theft, or natural disasters. Liability insurance provides protection against legal claims and lawsuits, shielding personal assets from potential liabilities.

Estate planning emerges as another crucial aspect of managing wealth, ensuring the orderly distribution of assets according to one's wishes after death. This encompasses drafting a comprehensive will that outlines the distribution of assets, establishing trusts to manage and protect assets, and designating beneficiaries for retirement accounts and life insurance policies. By minimizing estate taxes through strategic planning, individuals can preserve more of their wealth for future generations. Asset allocation plays a pivotal role in wealth management, involving the strategic distribution of investments across various asset classes to achieve a balance between risk and return. Diversification helps reduce portfolio risk by spreading investments across different asset classes with varying risk profiles.

Building an emergency fund is paramount for protecting wealth and providing financial security in times of unexpected expenses or income disruptions. Aim to save three to six months' worth of living expenses in a readily accessible account to cover emergencies without jeopardizing long-term financial goals. Long-term investment strategies focused on wealth preservation and growth are essential for building and protecting wealth over time. Setting clear investment goals, regularly reviewing and rebalancing portfolios, and staying disciplined during market fluctuations are key components of a successful investment strategy.

Tax planning plays a crucial role in wealth management, with tax-efficient strategies helping minimize tax liabilities and preserve wealth. Maximize contributions to tax-advantaged retirement accounts, harvest investment losses to offset gains, and take advantage of tax deductions and credits. Implementing asset protection strategies can shield wealth from potential creditors, lawsuits, or other legal risks. This may involve structuring assets within legal entities such as trusts, limited liability companies (LLCs), or corporations, as well as purchasing liability insurance to protect personal assets.

Regular review and monitoring of financial plans and investment portfolios are crucial for identifying changes in circumstances or risks that may require adjustments. Stay informed about economic and market conditions and be prepared to adapt strategies accordingly to preserve and protect wealth effectively. By implementing these comprehensive strategies for protecting and preserving wealth, individuals can safeguard their financial well-being and achieve long-term financial security for themselves and future generations. Consultation with financial advisors and legal professionals is essential to develop a customized wealth management plan tailored to individual needs and circumstances.

A Millionaires Wealth and Risk Management Tactics

Millionaires employ a myriad of sophisticated strategies to manage their wealth and mitigate risks effectively, ensuring the preservation and growth of their financial assets. One of the key principles guiding their approach is diversification, which involves spreading investments across a range of asset classes to minimize exposure to any single risk. By diversifying their portfolios, millionaires can hedge against market volatility and reduce the impact of downturns in specific sectors or industries. They understand the importance of balancing risk and return, opting for a mix of conservative and aggressive investments based on their financial goals and risk tolerance. Moreover, millionaires prioritize long-term wealth accumulation over short-term gains, adopting a patient and disciplined approach to investing.

Asset allocation is a cornerstone of wealth management for millionaires, with careful consideration given to the allocation of investments across stocks, bonds, real estate, and alternative assets. They recognize that different asset classes perform differently under various market conditions and adjust their allocations accordingly to optimize returns while managing risk. Millionaires also leverage tax-efficient strategies to minimize tax liabilities and maximize after-tax returns on their investments. This may involve taking advantage of tax-deferred retirement accounts, capital gains harvesting, and strategic estate planning to minimize estate taxes.

Furthermore, millionaires are diligent in protecting their wealth from potential threats and liabilities. They invest in comprehensive insurance coverage to safeguard against unforeseen events such as accidents, illnesses, natural disasters, and lawsuits. By transferring risk to insurance companies, millionaires shield their assets and financial well-being from significant losses. Estate planning is another critical aspect of wealth management for millionaires, ensuring the orderly distribution of assets according to their wishes and minimizing estate taxes for future generations. They work with estate planning professionals to draft wills, establish trusts, and designate beneficiaries for retirement accounts and life insurance policies.

Millionaires also prioritize liquidity, maintaining a portion of their wealth in easily accessible cash reserves to cover expenses and seize investment opportunities as they arise. They understand the importance of having a financial safety net in place to weather economic downturns or unexpected expenses without disrupting their long-term financial goals. Moreover, millionaires actively seek out opportunities to generate passive income streams, such as rental properties, dividend-paying stocks, royalties, and royalties. By diversifying their income sources, they create a steady flow of cash flow that adds stability to their financial portfolios.

In addition to prudent financial management, millionaires invest in themselves through continuous education, self-improvement, and professional development. They understand that knowledge is power and actively seek out opportunities to expand their skills and expertise in various areas, including finance, entrepreneurship, and personal development. By staying informed and adaptable, millionaires can navigate changing market conditions and capitalize on emerging opportunities to grow their wealth.

Overall, millionaires manage their wealth and risk with a combination of strategic planning, disciplined investing, and prudent decision-making. By employing a diversified investment approach, leveraging tax-efficient strategies, protecting their assets, prioritizing liquidity, generating passive income, and investing in self-improvement, millionaires can achieve long-term financial success and security for themselves and future generations.

Everyday working people:

For everyday working people just starting to build their financial future, managing money and risk effectively is essential for long-term financial security and stability. Here's how they can do it:

1. Create a Budget: Start by creating a budget that outlines your income, expenses, and savings goals. This helps you track where your money is going and identify areas where you can cut back or save more.

2. Set Financial Goals: Define specific, achievable financial goals that give you direction and motivation. Whether it's saving for an emergency fund, paying off debt, or investing for retirement, having clear goals helps you stay focused on your financial priorities.

3. Build an Emergency Fund: Start by building an emergency fund to cover unexpected expenses or income disruptions. Aim to save three to six months' worth of living expenses in a readily accessible account.

4. Pay Off High-Interest Debt: Prioritize paying off high-interest debt such as credit card balances or personal loans. Focus on paying more than the minimum payment each month to accelerate debt repayment and save on interest.

5. Start Investing Early: Take advantage of compound interest by starting to invest early, even if it's just a small amount. Consider investing in tax-advantaged retirement accounts such as a 401(k) or IRA to maximize long-term growth potential.

6. Diversify Investments: Spread your investments across different asset classes and industries to reduce risk. This helps cushion the impact of market fluctuations and potential losses in any one investment.

7. Educate Yourself: Take the time to educate yourself about personal finance and investment principles. There are plenty of resources available, including books, online courses, and financial websites, to help you improve your financial literacy.

8. Seek Professional Advice: Consider consulting with a financial advisor or planner to help you develop a personalized financial plan tailored to your goals and circumstances. They can provide valuable guidance and expertise to help you make informed decisions.

9. Protect Your Assets: Invest in insurance coverage to protect yourself and your assets from unforeseen events such as accidents, illnesses, or natural disasters. This includes health insurance, life insurance, disability insurance, and property and casualty insurance.

10. Stay Flexible: Be prepared to adapt your financial plan as your circumstances change or unexpected events occur. Flexibility is key to navigating life's ups and downs and staying on track towards your financial goals.

11. Avoid Impulse Spending: Practice discipline by avoiding unnecessary purchases or impulse spending. Before making a purchase, ask yourself if it aligns with your financial goals and priorities.

12. Monitor Your Progress: Regularly review your financial plan and track your progress towards your goals. This helps you stay accountable and make adjustments as needed to stay on track.

13. Celebrate Milestones: Acknowledge and celebrate your financial achievements along the way, whether it's paying off debt, reaching a savings goal, or achieving a milestone in your investment portfolio. Celebrating your progress helps keep you motivated and focused on your financial journey.

14. Stay Patient and Persistent: Building wealth takes time and persistence, so stay patient and keep working towards your goals, even when progress seems slow. Remember that every small step forward brings you closer to financial freedom and security.

15. Stay Positive: Maintain a positive attitude and mindset, even in the face of challenges or setbacks. Focus on the progress you've made and the opportunities ahead, rather than dwelling on past mistakes or setbacks.

By following these strategies and staying disciplined and focused on your financial goals, everyday working people can effectively manage their money and risk, paving the way for a more secure and prosperous financial future.

Minimizing Risk Trading Stocks

When trading in the stock market, managing risk effectively is crucial to protect capital and maximize returns. Here are some of the best ways to manage risk:

1. Set Stop Loss Orders: Utilize stop loss orders to automatically sell a stock when it reaches a predetermined price, limiting potential losses. This helps prevent emotional decision-making and ensures that losses are kept within acceptable limits.

2. Diversify Your Portfolio: Spread investments across different asset classes, industries, and geographic regions to reduce exposure to any single risk. Diversification helps mitigate the impact of adverse events affecting individual stocks or sectors.

3. Perform Due Diligence: Conduct thorough research and analysis before making investment decisions. This includes studying company fundamentals, analyzing financial statements, assessing industry trends, and staying informed about macroeconomic factors that could impact the market.

4. Manage Position Sizes: Avoid overexposure to any single position by managing position sizes relative to the overall size of your portfolio. This helps minimize the impact of losses on the overall portfolio and reduces the risk of significant drawdowns.

5. Use Risk Management Tools: Take advantage of risk management tools such as position sizing calculators, volatility measures, and risk-reward ratios to assess the potential risk of each trade and make informed decisions.

6. Stay Informed: Keep abreast of market news, developments, and events that could impact stock prices. Stay informed about earnings reports, economic indicators, geopolitical events, and regulatory changes that could affect market sentiment.

7. Have a Trading Plan: Develop a clear trading plan that outlines your investment goals, risk tolerance, entry and exit criteria, and trading strategies. Stick to your plan and avoid making impulsive decisions based on emotion or speculation.

8. Monitor Your Trades: Regularly monitor your trades and adjust your strategies as needed based on changing market conditions. Be prepared to cut losses quickly if a trade is not performing as expected, and let winners run when they are profitable.

9. Stay Disciplined: Maintain discipline and consistency in your trading approach. Avoid chasing after hot tips or trying to time the market, as this often leads to poor decision-making and increased risk.

10. Review and Learn from Mistakes: Analyze your trading performance regularly and learn from both successes and failures. Identify areas for improvement and adjust your strategies accordingly to become a more successful and disciplined trader over time.

With these risk management techniques, traders can minimize potential losses, protect capital, and increase the likelihood of achieving long-term success in the stock market. Remember that trading involves inherent risks, and there are no guarantees of profits, but effective risk management can significantly improve the odds of success.

Common Pitfalls to avoid in wealth management

In wealth management, there are several common pitfalls that individuals should be aware of and strive to avoid. These pitfalls can hinder financial progress and jeopardize long-term wealth accumulation. Here are some of the most common pitfalls:

1. **Lack of Financial Planning:** Failing to establish clear financial goals and develop a comprehensive financial plan is a significant pitfall. Without a roadmap, individuals may struggle to prioritize their spending, saving, and investing activities, leading to inefficiencies, and missed opportunities for wealth accumulation.

2. **Overleveraging:** Taking on too much debt or using excessive leverage to finance investments can amplify losses and increase financial risk. It's essential to maintain a prudent level of debt and avoid overextending oneself financially.

3. **Neglecting Emergency Savings:** Not having an adequate emergency fund to cover unexpected expenses or income disruptions is a common pitfall. Without a financial safety net, individuals may be forced to resort to high-interest debt or liquidate investments prematurely, undermining long-term wealth-building efforts.

4. **Chasing Fads and Speculative Investments:** Succumbing to the temptation of chasing hot investment trends or speculative opportunities can lead to poor investment decisions and significant losses. It's crucial to conduct thorough research and exercise caution when evaluating investment opportunities.

5. **Failing to Diversify:** Overconcentration in a single asset class, sector, or investment can expose individuals to unnecessary risk. Diversification

helps spread risk across a range of assets and can mitigate the impact of adverse events on overall portfolio performance.

6. Market Timing: Attempting to time the market by buying and selling investments based on short-term fluctuations is a risky endeavor. Market timing strategies often result in missed opportunities and underperformance compared to a disciplined, long-term investment approach.

7. Ignoring Tax Implications: Failing to consider the tax implications of investment decisions can result in missed opportunities for tax savings and increased tax liabilities. It's essential to implement tax-efficient investment strategies and optimize tax-deferred accounts to maximize after-tax returns.

8. Emotional Decision-Making: Allowing emotions such as fear, greed, or overconfidence to drive investment decisions can lead to impulsive actions and suboptimal outcomes. It's crucial to remain disciplined and rational, sticking to a well-thought-out investment plan regardless of market fluctuations or external influences.

9. Ignoring Estate Planning: Neglecting to establish an estate plan can result in unintended consequences for the distribution of assets and estate taxes. It's important to create a will, establish trusts, and designate beneficiaries to ensure that assets are transferred according to one's wishes and minimize estate tax liabilities.

10. Failing to Review and Adjust: Neglecting to periodically review and adjust financial plans and investment portfolios can lead to suboptimal outcomes. It's essential to regularly assess progress towards financial goals, evaluate investment performance, and make adjustments as needed based on changing circumstances or objectives.

By avoiding these common pitfalls and adopting sound wealth management practices, individuals can enhance their financial well-being and achieve long-term success in building and preserving wealth. Consulting with financial professionals and staying informed about best practices in wealth management can help individuals navigate potential pitfalls and make informed decisions to achieve their financial goals.

Michael's journey exemplifies the power of knowledge, mentorship, and disciplined investing in managing wealth and risk effectively. Through reading books and seeking guidance from mentors, he gained valuable insights and strategies for navigating the stock market and building wealth over time. One such strategy he embraced was dollar-cost averaging, which involves regularly investing a fixed amount of money into the market regardless of its fluctuations. By consistently purchasing stocks, even during market downturns, Michael was able to capitalize on lower prices and accumulate shares over time. He understood that while markets may experience temporary declines, they historically tend to recover and grow over the long term.

Moreover, Michael's commitment to contributing to his company 401(k) during down markets further exemplifies his disciplined approach to wealth management. By continuing to invest, especially when stock prices were low, he took advantage of dollar-cost averaging within his retirement account as well. Additionally, leveraging his company's matching contributions provided an extra boost to his retirement savings, further enhancing his long-term financial security.

Michael's story serves as a reminder to everyday working individuals striving to build for the future. Despite inevitable market fluctuations and economic uncertainties, staying the course and remaining committed to a sound investment strategy is paramount. By maintaining a long-term perspective and not succumbing to fear or panic during market downturns, individuals can weather temporary setbacks and ultimately achieve their financial goals. As the adage goes, "troubles don't last always," and by persevering through both good times and bad, individuals can emerge stronger and more resilient in the end. Through disciplined saving, investing, and staying true to their financial plans, individuals like Michael can pave the way for a more secure and prosperous future for themselves and their loved ones.

Chapter 12: Giving Back and Paying It Forward

Chapter 12 delves into Michael's journey of giving back and paying it forward as he works tirelessly towards financial freedom. One of Michael's most cherished dreams is to give his mother a gift like no other. Initially, this dream wasn't even a consideration, but it became a poignant goal following the passing of Michael's father. Realizing that his mother was living alone in her current house, isolated from family and friends, Michael felt a deep sense of responsibility to improve her living situation even though his mom lived a decent life. It was Michael's wife, Amal, who planted the seed of this idea in his mind. Amal, a steadfast supporter of Michael, stood by his side through every endeavor, offering unwavering encouragement and belief in his capabilities.

Driven by his love for his mother and inspired by Amal's suggestion, Michael embarked on a mission to turn his dream into reality. He worked tirelessly, leveraging his financial knowledge and resources to continue to build wealth and create opportunities for himself and his loved ones. Michael understood that achieving financial freedom would not only benefit his own family but also enable him to make a meaningful difference in the lives of others.

With Amal's steadfast support and encouragement, Michael remained focused on his goals, navigating challenges and setbacks with determination and resilience. He remained committed to his vision of providing his mother with a new home, knowing that it would not only enhance her quality of life but also symbolize his gratitude and love for her.

As Michael's journey unfolded, he found fulfillment not only in achieving his own financial goals but also in giving back to others. He recognized the importance of paying it forward, using his success as a platform to uplift and support those in need. Through acts of generosity, kindness, and philanthropy, Michael demonstrated the profound impact that one person's dedication and compassion can have on the lives of others. Michael always gave to the homeless in many cities and countries he traveled too. Michael also gave to multiple charities along the way.

Michael's dream of giving his mother a new home serves as a testament to the power of love, determination, and generosity. It is a reminder that true wealth is not measured solely in monetary terms but also in the ability to make a positive difference in the lives of others. By giving back and paying it forward, Michael embodies the spirit of compassion and generosity, leaving a lasting legacy of kindness and goodwill for generations to come. Michael would continue planning with his Wife Amal to make this dream a reality. Time was on Michaels side, and he had learned to plan and be patient and strike at the precise time.

As we take a step back into time from Michaels early teenage years, Michael had always possessed a generous spirit. Despite his own limited resources, he never hesitated to extend a helping hand to those in need. Many remarked that Michael inherited this trait from his father, who was renowned for his selflessness. As Michael returned to the United States from Iraq and reconnected with childhood friends, he found himself surrounded by all the childhood memories that helped shape Michael into the individual he was today.

Childhood to adulthood friends and family Ben, Alorie, Calvin, Mark, Reuben, Darnel, Marcus, Reginald, Jermain, Chris, and Joe. Among these friends were his best of friends Sidney and Alonzo, two steadfast companions who acts as brothers, had been by Michael's side for over two decades. Sidney, in particular, had always been someone Michael could confide in since childhood, their bond transcending from childhood before elementary school to adulthood. While their paths diverged, both Michael and Sidney found success in their respective endeavors.

Alonzo, another close friend, mirrored Michael's generosity. Over the years, he had provided invaluable support to Michael during challenging times. Michael never forgot Alonzo's kindness, recognizing that it had prevented him from facing financial ruin. Little did Alonzo know that his act of giving had a profound impact on Michael's life trajectory, ultimately keeping him in a steady place and leading him to cross paths with Terry and embark on a transformative journey. Without this simple act of kindness from Alonzo, Michael could have been set on an alternate path.

Indeed, the act of giving has the power to change lives in an instant. Alonzo's altruism not only helped Michael in his time of need but also set him on a path towards greater financial stability and personal growth. As Michael reflects on his own experiences, he is reminded of the profound impact that generosity can have on both the giver and the recipient. Now, with a renewed sense of purpose, Michael is committed to paying it forward and making a difference in the lives of others, just as Alonzo once did for him. Michael regards Alonzo and Sidney as more than just a friend; he sees them as true brothers and a source of inspiration.

One of the most significant acts of generosity in the beginning of Michaels financial freedom run, occurred during one of Michael's visits home. Amidst a family gathering, Michael gathered everyone's attention and invited his mother to stand beside him. With heartfelt sincerity, Michael presented his mother with a check to fully pay off her car loan. This gesture was a monumental achievement for Michael and left his mother speechless with disbelief. The act of kindness lifted a burden from his mother's shoulders that had seemed insurmountable. Michael's ability to provide assistance to his mother in any circumstance and at any time underscored his commitment to supporting and caring for his family.

The importance of philanthropy and giving back to the community

Philanthropy and giving back to the community are essential pillars of a compassionate society. These acts of generosity not only uplift individuals in need but also contribute to the overall well-being of society. By giving back, individuals can address pressing social issues, support marginalized communities, and promote positive change. Moreover, philanthropy fosters a sense of interconnectedness and empathy, encouraging individuals to look beyond their own needs and consider the welfare of others. Whether through financial contributions, volunteer work, or advocacy efforts, each act of philanthropy has the power to make a meaningful difference in the lives of individuals and communities alike.

Furthermore, philanthropy benefits the giver as much as the recipient, fostering a sense of fulfillment, purpose, and connection to the broader community. Ultimately, by prioritizing philanthropy and giving back, individuals can create a more equitable and compassionate society for all.

Even for everyday regular working people with limited resources, finding ways to give back is both admirable and impactful. Michael's grandfather's wise words, "give a little, save a little, and you'll always have a little," resonate deeply, highlighting the importance of generosity and financial prudence. Michael never forgot these words when he was 16 years old. While it may seem daunting to give when finances are tight, even small acts of kindness can make a significant difference. Whether it's donating spare change, volunteering time, or offering support to those in need, every contribution matters. Michael's grandfather's advice reminds us that giving is not solely about the amount but rather the intention behind the gesture.

By prioritizing giving, individuals can cultivate a spirit of compassion and generosity that enriches both their own lives and the lives of others. Additionally, practicing prudent financial habits, such as saving alongside giving, ensures long-term sustainability and enables individuals to continue making a positive impact over time. Thus, even amidst life's challenges, finding ways to give back embodies the true essence of generosity and community spirit.

Millionaires, endowed with substantial resources and influence, often recognize the importance of giving back to their communities as a means to effect positive change for the less fortunate. They understand that their success is intertwined with the well-being of their community and feel a sense of responsibility to contribute to its betterment. Through philanthropy, millionaires support various initiatives, such as education, healthcare, poverty alleviation, and environmental conservation, among others. They establish charitable foundations, donate to causes aligned with their values, and actively participate in community development projects.

Additionally, many millionaires leverage their expertise and networks to mentor aspiring entrepreneurs, provide scholarships, or create job opportunities, thereby fostering economic empowerment and social mobility. By giving back, millionaires not only make tangible improvements in their communities but also inspire others to do the same, creating a ripple effect of generosity and compassion. In doing so, they leave a lasting legacy of positive impact and contribute to building a more equitable and thriving society for all.

How Companies Gives Back Through Dividends

Companies often give back to their investors through dividends, which are payments made to shareholders from the company's earnings. Dividends are a way for companies to share their profits with investors as a reward for their ownership of the company's stock. One example of how a company can pay dividends is by declaring a dividend per share amount, which is then distributed to shareholders on a regular basis, usually quarterly or annually.

For instance, let's consider a fictional company, XYZ Inc., which has had a profitable year. The company's board of directors meets and decides to declare a dividend of $0.50 per share to be paid out to shareholders. If an investor owns 100 shares of XYZ Inc. stock, they would receive a dividend payment of $50 (100 shares x $0.50 per share).

Companies typically announce their dividend payments along with the declaration date, ex-dividend date, record date, and payment date. The declaration date is when the company's board of directors announces its intention to pay a dividend. The ex-dividend date is the first day the stock trades without the dividend, and investors who purchase the stock on or after this date are not entitled to receive the upcoming dividend payment. The record date is the date on which shareholders must be on the company's books to receive the dividend, and the payment date is when the dividend is actually paid to shareholders.

By paying dividends, companies can attract and retain investors who seek income from their investments. Dividend payments can also signal a company's financial health and stability, as consistent or increasing dividends indicate confidence in the company's future earnings potential. Overall, dividends provide a tangible way for companies to give back to their investors and reward them for their investment in the company's success.

How your employer gives back through 401k match programs

Employers often give back to their employees through company 401(k) matches, which are contributions made by the employer to an employee's retirement savings account based on the employee's contributions. This is a valuable benefit that helps employees save for their future and build a retirement nest egg.

An example of how a company can offer a 401(k) match is as follows: Let's say an employer decides to match 50% of an employee's contributions, up to a certain percentage of the employee's salary. For instance, if an employee contributes 6% of their salary to their 401(k) plan, the employer will match half of that contribution, contributing an additional 3% of the employee's salary to their retirement savings account.

Here's how it works in practice:

- If an employee earns $50,000 per year and contributes 6% of their salary to their 401(k), which amounts to $3,000 annually.
- With a 50% match, the employer would contribute an additional 3% of the employee's salary, which is $1,500 per year.
- In total, the employee would have $4,500 contributed to their 401(k) account annually ($3,000 from their own contributions and $1,500 from the employer's match).

Employers may have different matching formulas and contribution limits, but the goal is to incentivize employees to save for retirement by offering additional funds to bolster their retirement savings. This benefit not only helps employees build wealth for their future but also fosters loyalty and satisfaction among the workforce, as they feel supported and valued by their employer.

Ways regular everyday people can give back and pay it forward:

1. Volunteer at local charities or nonprofit organizations.

2. Donate clothing, household items, or food to shelters or community centers.

3. Offer to help elderly neighbors with household chores or errands.

4. Mentor a young person or offer tutoring services to students in need.

5. Participate in community clean-up events or environmental conservation projects.

6. Support small businesses and artisans by shopping locally or buying handmade goods.

7. Organize a fundraiser or charity event for a cause you're passionate about.

8. Participate in blood drives or donate blood to help those in need of transfusions.

9. Visit nursing homes or hospitals to spend time with residents or patients.

10. Share your skills or expertise by offering free workshops or classes in your community.

11. Support crowdfunding campaigns for individuals or families facing financial hardships.

12. Write letters of appreciation to frontline workers, teachers, or military personnel.

13. Volunteer at animal shelters or foster pets in need of temporary homes.

14. Organize a neighborhood food drive to collect donations for local food banks.

15. Participate in community gardening projects to provide fresh produce for those in need.

16. Advocate for social justice and equality by participating in peaceful protests or awareness campaigns.

17. Volunteer at local schools or libraries to help children improve their literacy skills.

18. Participate in fundraising walks, runs, or bike rides for charities or research organizations.

19. Donate unused frequent flyer miles or hotel points to organizations that provide travel assistance to those in need.

20. Offer your time and expertise to assist individuals or families with financial planning or budgeting.

These are just a few examples of how regular everyday people can make a positive impact in their communities and beyond by giving back and paying it forward. No matter how big or small your contribution may seem, every act of kindness has the power to make a difference in someone's life.

No matter the size or scope of our actions, finding a way to give back and pay it forward can have a profound and lasting impact on both individuals and communities. Sometimes, it's easy to feel overwhelmed by the enormity of the world's problems and to believe that our individual efforts won't make a difference. However, it's essential to recognize that even the smallest acts of kindness and generosity can ripple outward, creating positive change far beyond their initial impact. Whether it's volunteering at a local shelter, donating clothing to those in need, or simply offering a listening ear to someone going through a difficult time, every gesture of compassion and goodwill has the potential to brighten someone's day and restore their hope and faith in humanity.

These seemingly small acts can also inspire others to follow suit, creating a domino effect of kindness and generosity that reverberates throughout society. Moreover, the benefits of giving back and paying it forward extend beyond the immediate recipients of our actions. Research has shown that acts of kindness and altruism can boost our own well-being and sense of fulfillment, leading to greater levels of happiness and life satisfaction. By contributing to the greater good, we not only enrich the lives of others but also enrich our own lives in the process. Furthermore, the impact of our actions often extends far into the future, shaping the world we leave behind for future generations.

Whether it's planting trees to combat climate change, supporting educational initiatives to empower underserved communities, or advocating for social justice and equality, our efforts today can lay the foundation for a brighter and more equitable tomorrow. In essence, it's not the size or grandeur of our deeds that matters most, but the intention and sincerity behind them. By finding ways to give back and pay it forward, we can all play a part in creating a more compassionate, inclusive, and harmonious world for ourselves and for generations to come. As the saying goes, "No act of kindness, no matter how small, is ever wasted."

Michaels Act of Kindness and Giving:

Michael always believed in the transformative power of kindness, understanding that acts of generosity had the potential to impact both the giver and the receiver in profound ways. For Michael, one such act of kindness was a deeply personal mission—to provide his mother with the gift of a new home. Together with his wife, Amal, Michael embarked on a journey to find the perfect home for his mother—a place that would offer comfort, security, and a sense of belonging.

The search for the ideal home was no easy task, requiring Michael and Amal to scour countless listings, visit numerous properties, and navigate the intricacies of the real estate market. But despite the challenges, they remained steadfast in their determination, knowing that patience would ultimately lead them to the right place.

After months of searching, Michael and Amal stumbled upon a home that seemed to check all the boxes—a charming house in the perfect location, priced within their budget. Without hesitation, Michael reached out to his real estate agent and made an offer slightly above the asking price, confident that this home was worth every penny.

However, their initial excitement was dampened when they learned that the house had already been placed under contract with another buyer. Undeterred, Michael persisted, following up with the realtor in the hopes that circumstances might change. And change they did—several weeks later, Michael received the news he had been waiting for: the contract had fallen through, and the owners had accepted his offer.

With the deal finalized and the appraisal confirming the value of the home, Michael and Amal eagerly set a date to surprise his mother with the news. But fate had other plans—just as they were preparing to travel home, tragedy struck. Michael's mother lost her oldest brother to cancer, casting a shadow over their plans and turning their visit into a somber affair.

Despite the heartbreaking loss, Michael and Amal remained determined to lift his mother's spirits, recognizing that the gift of a new home would serve as a beacon of hope amidst the darkness. They extended their visit, using the extra time to replan the unveiling of the surprise, hoping to bring some joy to his grieving family.

A dinner gathering was arranged, bringing together Michael's mother and her siblings in a bittersweet moment of togetherness. As the evening unfolded, Michael, Amal, and his sister Valerie presented the keys to the new home, along with flowers and a framed picture—a gesture that left his mother and the entire family speechless.

Overwhelmed with emotion, Michael's mother broke down in tears of gratitude and disbelief, her joy mirrored by the tears of her siblings and cousins. Together, they visited the new home, marveling at the love and generosity that had made it possible.

In the end, Michael's act of kindness transcended the boundaries of his immediate family, touching the hearts of all who witnessed it in that restaurant that day. Strangers cried and gave their support on a job well done as they found out what had happened. It was a testament to the power of love, compassion, and selflessness—a reminder that even in the darkest of times, the light of kindness has the power to illuminate our lives and bring hope to those in need.

Michael's mother's unwavering support for his decision to go to Iraq, despite her concerns, set in motion a series of events that culminated in this significant moment. This pivotal decision ultimately led Michael and his wife Amal to present one of the most meaningful gifts: a new home. This home was strategically located to be 5 minutes away from her brother's and sisters in a new city, this allowed the family to be together and support each other in good and bad times. This act of generosity embodies the essence of giving and paying it forward.

After accomplishing all of this, Michael thought of other ways to give back and then took the initiative to assist his mother in renting out her older home, thereby creating a source of monthly income for her. Once this task was successfully accomplished, Michael had one final gift to offer his mother: the gift of financial freedom. In a heartwarming gesture, Michael retired his mother, ensuring that she could live her life freely and without financial worries.

Giving Back to Your Community

Michael and his family were always a big supporter of giving back to the local community. Mainly through gatherings and cookouts where they invited the entire neighborhood. These acts brought the neighborhood together. In earlier days, each year for thanksgiving Michaels mother and father would host a turkey frying event for anyone in the neighborhood. This event allowed people to bring their thanksgiving turkeys and have them fried for free. This too brought friends and family members together to socialize and spend time together, building stronger relationships and bonds.

In addition to Michael's commitment to giving back to his local community, Michael extended his philanthropic efforts to the military personnel and civilian workers in Iraq. Recognizing the importance of fostering camaraderie and support among those serving in the war-torn country, Michael initiated a bi-weekly event aimed at bringing everyone together for a cookout. The event was called the "The Tomahawk Jam". Tomahawk village is where Michael and his coworkers lived and thought it would be a great idea to name the event after the village and to bring the people to that location.

This initiative quickly gained momentum, with each event attracting more than a hundred participants from diverse backgrounds and nationalities. Through these gatherings, Michael created a space for people to come together, unwind, and forge meaningful connections amidst the challenges of wartime.

Beyond simply providing a meal, these cookouts served as a platform for individuals to share their experiences, stories, and insights. Michael gained valuable perspectives on culture, daily life, and resilience from the diverse group of attendees, fostering a deeper understanding and appreciation for the human experience in Iraq.

Moreover, the bonds formed at these events transcended the confines of the war zone, leading to lasting friendships that endured long after Michael's time in Iraq. The sense of community and solidarity cultivated through these gatherings left a lasting impact on all who attended, providing a source of comfort, support, and camaraderie in an otherwise challenging environment.

Through his commitment to fostering connections and supporting those serving alongside him, Michael exemplified the spirit of generosity and compassion, demonstrating the transformative power of giving back to others, even in the most challenging of circumstances.

Chapter 13: Navigating Success and Its Challenges

Navigating Success and Its Challenges, we revisit the journey of Michael, reflecting on the myriad challenges he encountered and overcame on his path to success. From his early days as a struggling teenager to his eventual triumphs as an investor and philanthropist, Michael's story is riddled with obstacles that tested his resolve. Despite facing financial hardships, familial responsibilities, and the rigors of supporting our military service members in a war-torn country, Michael persevered with unwavering determination.

Throughout his life, Michael encountered setbacks and failures that could have derailed his progress. From the loss of loved ones to financial struggles and personal doubts, he weathered storms that threatened to extinguish his dreams. Yet, with each adversity, Michael emerged stronger and more resilient, refusing to succumb to despair. Instead, he used these challenges as opportunities for growth, learning valuable lessons that would shape his future success.

In the face of adversity, Michael remained steadfast in his pursuit of excellence. He embraced failure as a necessary steppingstone on the path to greatness, understanding that success often requires perseverance in the face of adversity. With each setback, Michael recalibrated his approach, refining his strategies and honing his skills to overcome obstacles with renewed determination.

Despite the daunting challenges he faced, Michael refused to let fear or self-doubt hold him back. Instead, he embraced the unknown with courage and optimism, viewing every obstacle as a chance to prove his resilience and determination. Through hard work, perseverance, and unwavering faith in his abilities, Michael navigated the complexities of life with grace and determination, emerging victorious in the face of adversity.

In the end, Michael's journey serves as a testament to the power of resilience, determination, and unwavering faith in the face of adversity. His story reminds us that success is not defined by the absence of challenges but by our ability to overcome them with courage and conviction. By embracing the inevitable ups and downs of life, we can navigate the path to success with resilience and grace, emerging stronger and more triumphant than ever before.

Navigating the challenges and responsibilities that accompany wealth and success can be a daunting task for anyone, regardless of their background or circumstances. For everyday people, achieving financial success often comes with its own set of challenges, including managing debt, balancing work and family obligations, and planning for the future. However, with careful planning, discipline, and perseverance, these challenges can be overcome.

Regular Working Individuals

One of the primary challenges faced by individuals striving for success is managing newfound wealth responsibly. Without proper financial literacy and discipline, sudden windfalls or increases in income can quickly lead to overspending, debt accumulation, and ultimately financial ruin. To overcome this challenge, it's essential for individuals to prioritize financial education and develop sound money management skills. This may involve creating a budget, living within one's means, and investing wisely for the future.

Another challenge associated with success is the pressure to maintain a certain lifestyle or standard of living. As individuals climb the ladder of success, there is often a temptation to indulge in luxury purchases or extravagant experiences. However, succumbing to this pressure can lead to lifestyle inflation and financial instability in the long run. Instead, it's important for individuals to remain grounded and prioritize long-term financial security over short-term gratification.

Millionaires

For millionaires, the challenges and responsibilities of wealth are amplified. In addition to managing their own finances, they may also have to navigate complex investment portfolios, oversee business ventures, and fulfill philanthropic obligations. Despite these challenges, successful millionaires often share common traits such as resilience, adaptability, and a willingness to seek advice from trusted advisors. Millionaires also have a team that plays a viable role in supporting these efforts.

To continue their millionaire status, successful individuals must remain vigilant in managing their wealth and mitigating risks. This may involve diversifying their investment portfolio, staying abreast of market trends, and adjusting their strategies as needed. Additionally, millionaires have a responsibility to give back to their communities and contribute to the greater good. By leveraging their resources and influence for philanthropic endeavors, they can make a positive impact on society while also solidifying their legacy.

Navigating the challenges and responsibilities of wealth and success requires careful planning, discipline, and resilience. Whether you're an everyday person striving for financial stability or a millionaire seeking to preserve your wealth, overcoming challenges and fulfilling responsibilities requires a proactive approach and a commitment to long-term success. By prioritizing financial literacy, prudent decision-making, and giving back to others, individuals can achieve lasting prosperity and make a meaningful impact on the world around them.

Challenges of Wealth and Success

1. Managing Finances: With increased wealth comes the responsibility of managing larger sums of money. This includes budgeting, investing, and minimizing expenses to ensure long-term financial stability.

Overcoming: Seek financial education, create a detailed budget, diversify investments, and regularly review financial goals and strategies.

2. Lifestyle Inflation: The temptation to increase spending as income rises can lead to lifestyle inflation, where expenses outpace income growth, potentially derailing financial plans.

Overcoming: Practice conscious spending, avoid unnecessary luxuries, and focus on long-term financial goals rather than short-term gratification.

3. Risk Management: Wealth accumulation often involves taking risks, whether through investments, business ventures, or other opportunities. However, excessive risk-taking can result in significant losses.

Overcoming: Diversify investments to spread risk, conduct thorough due diligence before making financial decisions, and consider consulting with financial advisors.

4. Family Dynamics: Family relationships and expectations can be affected by wealth, leading to conflicts over inheritances, financial support, or differing lifestyles.

Overcoming: Establish open communication with family members, set clear boundaries, and seek professional guidance when addressing sensitive family issues.

5. Public Scrutiny: High-profile individuals may face public scrutiny and pressure to maintain a certain image or lifestyle, which can be stressful and intrusive.

Overcoming: Focus on personal values and priorities, maintain authenticity, and surround yourself with a supportive network of friends and advisors.

6. Legal and Tax Considerations: Increased wealth often entails complex legal and tax implications, requiring careful planning and compliance with regulations.

Overcoming: Consult with legal and tax professionals to develop comprehensive strategies for asset protection, estate planning, and tax optimization.

7. Philanthropic Obligations: Wealthy individuals may feel a sense of responsibility to give back to their communities or support charitable causes, which requires time, resources, and strategic decision-making.

Overcoming: Identify causes that align with personal values and interests, establish clear philanthropic goals, and leverage resources effectively to maximize impact.

8. Maintaining Work-Life Balance: Success can consume significant time and energy, leading to burnout and neglect of personal relationships or well-being.

Overcoming: Prioritize self-care, establish boundaries between work and personal life, and delegate tasks when possible, to maintain balance and prevent burnout.

9. Legacy Planning: As wealth accumulates, individuals may grapple with questions of legacy and how to ensure their wealth has a meaningful and lasting impact beyond their lifetime.

Overcoming: Develop a comprehensive estate plan, including wills, trusts, and charitable giving strategies, to ensure assets are distributed according to personal wishes and values.

10. Social Isolation: Wealth and success can sometimes lead to feelings of isolation or disconnect from peers or community members who may not share the same financial circumstances.

Overcoming: Cultivate genuine relationships based on shared interests and values rather than financial status, seek opportunities for community engagement and social connection, and consider joining peer networks or support groups for like-minded individuals.

Responsibilities of Wealth and Success

1. Financial Stewardship: Managing wealth responsibly involves making informed financial decisions, protecting assets, and planning for the future.

Overcoming: Educate yourself on financial management principles, regularly review financial statements, and seek professional advice when needed.

2. Charitable Giving: With financial success comes the opportunity to give back to others through philanthropy and charitable contributions.

Overcoming: Identify causes or organizations that align with your values, establish a charitable giving plan, and allocate resources effectively to maximize impact.

3. Family Support: Wealth can bring expectations from family members for financial assistance or support, requiring careful navigation of family dynamics.

Overcoming: Set clear boundaries and expectations with family members, communicate openly about financial matters, and provide support in ways that empower rather than enable.

4. Leadership and Mentorship: Successful individuals may have a responsibility to share their knowledge and experience with others, whether through mentorship, coaching, or leadership roles.

Overcoming: Seek opportunities to mentor or guide others, share insights and lessons learned from your own journey, and lead by example in both personal and professional endeavors.

5. Corporate Social Responsibility: Wealthy individuals who own or lead businesses have a responsibility to operate ethically, contribute to their communities, and minimize negative social or environmental impacts.

Overcoming: Integrate social and environmental considerations into business practices, support sustainable initiatives, and engage with stakeholders to address concerns and promote positive change.

6. Civic Engagement: Success may bring opportunities for civic involvement and advocacy on issues of importance to society, requiring active participation in public affairs.

Overcoming: Stay informed about local and national issues, participate in community events and organizations, and use your platform or resources to advocate for positive change.

7. Estate Planning: Planning for the distribution of wealth after death is a critical responsibility for successful individuals to ensure assets are managed and transferred according to their wishes.

Overcoming: Work with legal and financial advisors to develop a comprehensive estate plan, including wills, trusts, and other tools for asset protection and succession planning.

8. Mentoring Future Generations: Wealthy individuals may have a responsibility to educate and mentor the next generation on financial literacy, entrepreneurship, and leadership.

Overcoming: Take an active role in mentoring family members or young professionals, share knowledge and expertise through workshops or seminars, and provide guidance on responsible money management and career development.

9. Environmental Sustainability: Success brings influence and resources that can be used to promote environmental conservation and sustainability efforts.

Overcoming: Implement eco-friendly practices in personal and professional life, support renewable energy initiatives, and advocate for policies that protect the environment and address climate change.

10. Personal Growth and Development: Alongside financial success comes the responsibility to continue learning, growing, and evolving as an individual.

Overcoming: Invest in personal development through education, self-reflection, and seeking new challenges or experiences, prioritize mental and physical well-being, and cultivate a growth mindset to adapt to changing circumstances.

The journey to millionaire status is not merely about accumulating wealth, but also about personal and professional growth. Throughout this journey, individuals experience transformation, both in terms of their mindset and their actions. They learn valuable lessons about financial management, resilience, and the importance of giving back to others.

Alongside the pursuit of wealth, individuals encounter various challenges and responsibilities that come with success. These include financial stewardship, charitable giving, family support, leadership, and corporate social responsibility. Overcoming these challenges requires careful planning, effective communication, and a commitment to ethical decision-making.

Ultimately, achieving millionaire status is not just about reaching a financial milestone; it's about becoming a better version of oneself. It's about embracing the responsibilities that come with success and using one's resources to make a positive impact on the world. By reflecting on their journey and embracing ongoing personal and professional growth, individuals can continue to thrive as they navigate the complexities of wealth and success. Michael learned through self-studies, through friendships, family, and mentorships. Surround yourself with the right people and you too can start your journey to millionaire status.

Chapter 14: Maintaining Work-Life Balance

Michael's journey towards achieving work-life balance has been a testament to perseverance and adaptation. In the early days, juggling a demanding night shift job, daytime college classes, and the responsibilities of fatherhood presented significant challenges. However, Michael was determined to find equilibrium in his life, prioritizing time with his young son on his days off while still meeting his professional and academic commitments.

Transitioning to overseas work brought its own set of challenges, but it also provided Michael with a newfound focus. Being away from family and friends allowed him to channel his energy into building a secure future for his loved ones. Despite the distance, Michael made it a priority to stay connected with his son, offering encouragement and support through regular communication.

Over time, Michael found a rhythm that worked for him, integrating work and personal life into a harmonious routine. This routine became essential in maintaining his bond with his son and other family members despite the physical distance. By embracing the challenges and embracing the opportunities that came with his work, Michael was able to achieve a sense of balance that allowed him to thrive both personally and professionally.

Maintaining balance and well-being is crucial, especially when pursuing financial goals. While it's essential to strive for success and financial stability, it's equally important to prioritize one's health and overall well-being. Here are some key reasons why maintaining balance is essential in the pursuit of financial goals:

The importance of maintaining balance and well-being amidst the pursuit of financial goals

1. **Physical Health:** Neglecting one's physical health in pursuit of financial goals can have detrimental effects. Stress, lack of exercise, and poor eating

habits can lead to various health issues, including obesity, heart disease, and mental health disorders.

2. Mental Health: Financial stress and overwork can take a toll on mental well-being. Anxiety, depression, and burnout are common consequences of neglecting self-care in favor of financial pursuits.

3. Quality of Life: Achieving financial success should enhance one's quality of life, not detract from it. Maintaining balance ensures that individuals have time and energy to enjoy life outside of work and financial endeavors.

4. Relationships: Neglecting relationships with family and friends in pursuit of financial goals can lead to feelings of isolation and loneliness. Strong social connections are vital for emotional well-being and can provide crucial support during challenging times.

5. Work Performance: Burnout and fatigue can negatively impact work performance, ultimately hindering progress towards financial goals. Maintaining balance allows individuals to remain focused, productive, and engaged in their professional endeavors.

6. Creativity and Innovation: Overwork and stress can stifle creativity and innovation. Taking time for rest and relaxation fosters a clear mind and allows for fresh perspectives, leading to more creative problem-solving and entrepreneurial ventures.

7. Long-Term Sustainability: A balanced approach to pursuing financial goals ensures long-term sustainability. Avoiding burnout and maintaining good health allows individuals to sustain their efforts over time, increasing the likelihood of achieving lasting success.

8. Setting Boundaries: Establishing boundaries between work, personal life, and financial pursuits is essential for maintaining balance. Learning to say no to excessive work demands and setting aside time for leisure activities is crucial for overall well-being.

9. Self-Care Practices: Incorporating self-care practices such as exercise, meditation, and hobbies into daily routines is essential for maintaining balance. These activities help reduce stress, improve mood, and promote overall health and well-being.

10. Financial Stability: Striving for balance does not mean neglecting financial goals. In fact, prioritizing self-care can lead to greater financial stability in the long run. Healthy individuals are better equipped to make sound financial decisions and adapt to economic challenges.

11. Time Management: Balancing work, personal life, and financial goals requires effective time management skills. Setting priorities, delegating tasks, and scheduling downtime are essential strategies for maintaining balance and avoiding burnout.

12. Adaptability: Life is unpredictable, and maintaining balance allows individuals to adapt to unexpected challenges and changes in circumstances. Flexibility and resilience are key traits that contribute to long-term success and well-being.

13. Reflection and Growth: Taking time for self-reflection and personal growth is an integral part of maintaining balance. Engaging in activities such as journaling, therapy, or self-improvement workshops fosters self-awareness and personal development.

14. Role Modeling: Prioritizing balance sets a positive example for others, including family members, colleagues, and friends. By demonstrating the importance of self-care and well-being, individuals inspire others to prioritize their health and happiness.

15. Preventing Burnout: Burnout is a significant risk when individuals neglect their well-being in pursuit of financial goals. Recognizing the signs of burnout, such as exhaustion, cynicism, and reduced performance, is essential for taking proactive steps to prevent it.

16. Work-Life Integration: Achieving balance does not always mean strict separation between work and personal life. Instead, it involves integrating work and personal responsibilities in a way that promotes overall well-being and fulfillment.

17. Financial Planning: Incorporating self-care and well-being into financial planning ensures a holistic approach to goal setting. Financial plans should prioritize both short-term financial objectives and long-term health and happiness.

18. Seeking Support: Maintaining balance often requires support from others. Seeking guidance from mentors, coaches, or therapists can provide valuable insights and strategies for achieving and maintaining balance.

19. Flexibility and Adaptation: Balance is not a static state but rather a dynamic process that requires ongoing adjustment and adaptation. Being flexible and willing to make changes as needed is essential for maintaining balance in the face of life's challenges.

20. Celebrating Milestones: Finally, it's essential to celebrate milestones and achievements along the journey to financial success. Recognizing progress and taking time to acknowledge accomplishments helps maintain motivation and perspective amidst the pursuit of long-term goals.

Tips for managing stress, prioritizing relationships, and enjoying life outside of work

Managing stress, prioritizing relationships, and enjoying life outside of work are essential components of maintaining balance and well-being. Here are some tips for achieving these goals:

1. Practice Mindfulness: Incorporate mindfulness practices such as meditation, deep breathing exercises, or yoga into your daily routine to reduce stress and promote relaxation.

2. Set Boundaries: Establish clear boundaries between work and personal life to prevent burnout. Designate specific times for work-related tasks and prioritize leisure activities and time spent with loved ones.

3. Delegate Responsibilities: Delegate tasks and responsibilities at work and home to lighten your load and reduce stress. Learn to trust others to handle certain tasks, allowing you to focus on priorities and enjoy downtime.

4. Prioritize Self-Care: Make self-care a priority by engaging in activities that nourish your mind, body, and soul. This could include exercise, hobbies, reading, or spending time outdoors.

5. Stay Connected: Nurture relationships with family and friends by scheduling regular quality time together. Make an effort to stay connected through phone calls, video chats, or in-person visits, even during busy periods.

6. Unplug Regularly: Take regular breaks from technology and screens to recharge and reconnect with the present moment. Set boundaries around device use, especially during leisure time and before bed.

7. Plan Leisure Activities: Schedule regular leisure activities and outings that bring you joy and fulfillment. Whether it's exploring nature, trying new hobbies, or attending cultural events, prioritize activities that make you happy.

8. Practice Gratitude: Cultivate an attitude of gratitude by focusing on the positive aspects of your life and expressing appreciation for the people and experiences that bring you joy. Keep a gratitude journal or share daily gratitude with loved ones.

9. Maintain Healthy Habits: Prioritize healthy habits such as getting enough sleep, eating nutritious foods, and staying hydrated. Physical well-being is closely linked to mental and emotional health, so prioritize self-care in all aspects of your life.

10. Seek Support: Don't hesitate to reach out for support from friends, family, or professional counselors when needed. Sharing your thoughts and feelings with others can provide valuable perspective and emotional support.

11. Set Realistic Goals: Avoid overcommitting yourself by setting realistic goals and expectations for work and personal life. Break larger tasks into smaller, manageable steps and celebrate progress along the way.

12. Learn to Say No: Practice assertiveness and learn to say no to commitments and obligations that don't align with your priorities or values. Protect your time and energy for activities and relationships that matter most to you.

13. Embrace Imperfection: Let go of perfectionism and embrace imperfection in yourself and others. Accept that life is unpredictable, and mistakes are a natural part of growth and learning.

14. Find Meaning and Purpose: Identify activities and pursuits that align with your values and bring a sense of meaning and purpose to your life. Engage in volunteer work, creative endeavors, or community involvement to contribute positively to the world around you.

15. Celebrate Small Wins: Acknowledge and celebrate small accomplishments and milestones along the way. Recognize your progress and give yourself credit for your efforts, no matter how small.

By incorporating these tips into your daily life, you can better manage stress, prioritize relationships, and find joy and fulfillment outside of work. Remember that balance is a journey, and it's essential to prioritize self-care and well-being along the way.

Michael's journey toward achieving work-life balance was marked by various strategies aimed at reducing stress and prioritizing his well-being. Amidst his busy schedule, Michael found solace in activities that allowed him to release stress and rejuvenate his mind and body. Traveling to new destinations provided him with opportunities to explore, unwind, and gain perspective outside of his everyday routine. Engaging in regular workouts not only improved his physical health but also served as a powerful outlet for releasing tension and boosting his mood.

Additionally, Michael discovered the benefits of quiet meditation and mindfulness practices, which helped him cultivate inner peace and clarity amidst life's challenges. By dedicating time each day to quiet reflection and mindfulness, he was able to quiet his mind, reduce stress levels, and regain a sense of balance and equilibrium. These practices became integral components of Michael's self-care routine, allowing him to navigate the demands of work and personal life with greater resilience and ease. By prioritizing activities that brought him joy and relaxation, Michael was able to sustain his well-being and foster a deeper connection with himself and those around him.

Ultimately, Michael's journey serves as a reminder of the importance of prioritizing self-care and finding healthy outlets for managing stress and maintaining balance in life. By incorporating travel, exercise, and mindfulness into his routine, Michael was able to cultivate a sense of fulfillment and happiness, even amidst life's challenges. Through these practices, he not only improved his overall well-being but also enhanced his capacity to navigate life's ups and downs with grace and resilience.

Chapter 15: Continuing the Journey

After leaving Iraq, Michael's journey took an unexpected turn when his company presented him with a new opportunity: relocating to Europe, specifically Stuttgart, Germany. This move opened doors to a world of exploration and adventure for Michael. Over the years spent in Germany, he immersed himself in the rich tapestry of European culture and used the opportunity to embark on extensive travels.

During his time in Germany, Michael's thirst for exploration led him to visit an astounding 40 different countries, each offering unique experiences and insights into diverse cultures. These travels broadened Michael's perspective and deepened his appreciation for the richness of human diversity.

But Michael's journey didn't end in Europe. His career eventually took him to Africa, where he continued to expand his horizons and explore new frontiers. It was during his time in Africa, while visiting Dubai in the United Arab Emirates, that Michael encountered an opportunity that would alter the course of his financial journey.

Walking through the bustling corridors of the Dubai mall, Michael was unexpectedly approached by representatives from a prominent property investment firm. Intrigued but initially skeptical, Michael decided to hear them out. As they outlined the potential benefits of investing in Dubai's rapidly growing economy through property investments, Michael's interest was piqued.

Despite his initial excitement, Michael was daunted by the prospect of investing in international markets, particularly one as dynamic and complex as Dubai. Determined to seize this opportunity, Michael and his wife, Amal, dedicated themselves to studying and understanding the intricacies of property investment in Dubai.

After months of diligent research and planning, Michael and Amal felt confident enough to take the plunge. They reached out to the investment firm and initiated the process of investing in Dubai's thriving real estate market. This decision marked a significant milestone in their journey towards financial prosperity and cemented their status as savvy investors willing to venture beyond familiar territories in pursuit of growth and success.

Michael and his wife wasted no time in capitalizing on the opportunity presented to them in Dubai. They returned to the city to meet with the investment firm once again, ready to take the next step in their financial journey. With careful consideration and meticulous planning, they paid the initial fees and proceeded to purchase their first property in Dubai.

Completing the transaction was just the beginning. Michael and Amal recognized the importance of effective property management, especially given the distance between their new investment and their home base. They entrusted a reputable property management company to oversee the rental of their property, ensuring a steady stream of income without the burden of day-to-day management.

The decision proved to be a lucrative one. Within months, their Dubai property began generating a substantial monthly income, exceeding their initial expectations. Buoyed by this success, Michael and Amal wasted no time in exploring further investment opportunities in the city.

As their confidence grew and their financial acumen sharpened, Michael and Amal made the bold decision to purchase a second property in Dubai. This strategic move proved to be the catalyst for their ascent to millionaire status, propelling them into a new realm of financial success and stability.

With multiple income streams flowing from their properties in Dubai, Michael and Amal found themselves on the fast track to achieving their long-term financial goals. Their journey from humble beginnings to millionaire status was a testament to their resilience, determination, and willingness to seize opportunities wherever they arose.

Continue your journey towards financial independence and lifelong learning!

As you continue on your journey towards financial independence, remember that it's not just about reaching a destination—it's about embracing the process of lifelong learning and personal growth. Each step you take, whether big or small, brings you closer to your goals and opens up new opportunities for success.

Embrace the mindset of continuous learning, staying curious, and seeking out new knowledge in areas that interest you. Whether it's exploring different investment strategies, honing your skills in budgeting, and saving, or delving into the intricacies of entrepreneurship, there's always something new to discover.

Stay open to new experiences and be willing to adapt to changing circumstances. Along the way, you may encounter setbacks and challenges, but these are valuable learning opportunities that can ultimately propel you forward. Remember that resilience and perseverance are key qualities on the path to financial independence.

Surround yourself with a supportive community of like-minded individuals who share your aspirations and values. Whether it's through networking events, online forums, or mentorship programs, connecting with others who are on a similar journey can provide valuable guidance, encouragement, and inspiration.

Above all, remain committed to your goals and stay focused on the vision you have for your future. By staying disciplined, making informed decisions, and taking consistent action, you'll continue to make progress towards financial independence and create a life of abundance and fulfillment. Keep moving forward, stay curious, and never stop learning— your journey towards financial freedom awaits!

Resources and further reading recommendations to support your ongoing growth and development:

1. Books on Personal Finance:

- "The Total Money Makeover" by Dave Ramsey

- "Rich Dad Poor Dad" by Robert T. Kiyosaki

- "The Millionaire Next Door" by Thomas J. Stanley and William D. Danko

- "Your Money or Your Life" by Vicki Robin and Joe Dominguez

- "The Intelligent Investor" by Benjamin Graham

2. Investing and Wealth Building:

 - "The Little Book of Common Sense Investing" by John C. Bogle

- "A Random Walk Down Wall Street" by Burton G. Malkiel

- "The Richest Man in Babylon" by George S. Clason

- "The Four Pillars of Investing" by William J. Bernstein

- "I Will Teach You to Be Rich" by Ramit Sethi

3. Entrepreneurship and Business:

- "The Lean Startup" by Eric Ries

- "Zero to One" by Peter Thiel and Blake Masters

- "The $100 Startup" by Chris Guillebeau

- "The E-Myth Revisited" by Michael E. Gerber

- "Start with Why" by Simon Sinek

4. Personal Development and Success:

- "Atomic Habits" by James Clear

- "Mindset: The New Psychology of Success" by Carol S. Dweck

- "The Power of Now" by Eckhart Tolle

- "The 7 Habits of Highly Effective People" by Stephen R. Covey

- "Thinking, Fast and Slow" by Daniel Kahneman

5. Online Courses and Educational Platforms:

- Coursera (www.coursera.org)

- Udemy (www.udemy.com)

- LinkedIn Learning (www.linkedin.com/learning)

- Khan Academy (www.khanacademy.org)

- Skill share (www.skillshare.com)

6. Financial Blogs and Websites:

- The Motley Fool (www.fool.com)

- Investopedia (www.investopedia.com)

- NerdWallet (www.nerdwallet.com)

- Mr. Money Mustache (www.mrmoneymustache.com)

- BiggerPockets (www.biggerpockets.com) - for real estate investing

7. Podcasts on Personal Finance and Investing:

- The Dave Ramsey Show

- The Tim Ferriss Show

- The Clark Howard Podcast

- The BiggerPockets Real Estate Podcast

- InvestED Podcast by Phil Town and Danielle Town

These resources cover a wide range of topics related to personal finance, investing, entrepreneurship, personal development, and more. Whether you prefer books, online courses, podcasts, or blogs, there's something here for everyone to continue their journey towards growth and success.

Michael's journey towards financial independence and unlocking his millionaire within was fueled by a thirst for knowledge and a commitment to self-education. Over the years, he dedicated himself to reading numerous books on personal finance, investing, entrepreneurship, podcasts, and wealth building. These books and podcasts also became his mentors, guiding him through the intricacies of financial management and providing valuable insights into the world of money.

Through the pages of these books, Michael learned about the importance of budgeting, saving, and investing wisely. He discovered various strategies for building wealth, from investing in stocks and real estate to starting his own business ventures. Each book offered a new perspective and valuable lessons that he could apply to his own financial journey.

As Michael delved deeper into the world of finance and investing, he began to develop a greater understanding of how money works and how he could make it work for him. He learned about the power of compound interest, the importance of diversification, and the value of long-term thinking.

But Michael didn't stop at just reading books—he actively applied the knowledge he gained to his own life. He created a financial plan, set goals, and took action to achieve them. He made smart decisions with his money, avoided unnecessary debt, and consistently invested in assets that would grow over time.

Through continuous learning and a commitment to self-improvement, Michael and his wife were able to unlock their millionaire lurking inside and achieve financial success. Their journey serves as a testament to the transformative power of education and the profound impact it can have on one's financial well-being.

As you continue your journey towards financial independence and lifelong learning, remember that the path to success is not always easy, but it is always worth it. By embracing the principles of financial management, investing wisely, and seeking opportunities for growth, you are laying the foundation for a brighter future. Keep striving, keep learning, and never underestimate the power of persistence and determination.

With the right mindset and the willingness to take action, you can achieve your goals and build the life you've always dreamed of. So, keep moving forward, stay focused on your objectives, and never stop pursuing your dreams. Your journey towards success is just beginning, and the possibilities are endless.

Chapter 16: Conclusion

In conclusion, "Unlocking the Millionaire Lurking Inside" serves as a guidebook for those seeking financial success and independence. Throughout its pages, readers are encouraged to adopt a mindset of abundance, embracing the belief that wealth is attainable through dedication and strategic action. The book emphasizes the importance of financial literacy, urging individuals to educate themselves about money management, investing, and entrepreneurship. It highlights the significance of diversifying income streams, showcasing various avenues such as real estate, stock market investments, and online businesses.

Moreover, the narrative underscores the value of giving back to the community, recognizing philanthropy as a means to create positive change and leave a lasting legacy. As readers embark on their journey towards wealth, the book reminds them to prioritize work-life balance, nurture relationships, and seek continual self-improvement. Ultimately, "Unlocking the Millionaire Lying Dormant Inside" concludes with the notion that success is not solely measured by monetary gains but by the fulfillment derived from living a purposeful and abundant life.

"Unlock the Millionaire Lying Dormant Inside" has also been a journey of discovery, growth, and transformation. Throughout the book, the exploration of the fundamental principles and strategies that can propel individuals towards financial success and independence.

Michael Final Story

As Michael's son Zyon transitioned into adulthood, embarking on his journey through college and the workforce, Michael recognized the importance of instilling financial responsibility in him from an early age. With this in mind, Michael took the initiative to help his son set up a personal brokerage account, allocating a modest monthly contribution of $150 towards automatic investments. Emphasizing the importance of patience and long-term growth, Michael encouraged his son to focus on the process rather than the immediate results, allowing his investments to flourish over time. Within just a year, Michael's son witnessed the remarkable growth of his investment account, with its value surpassing $2000.

This tangible evidence of the power of consistent, disciplined investing served as a testament to the wisdom of Michael's guidance. As Michael's son financial situation evolves and his income increases, he plans to further augment his contributions, laying the foundation for his on financial future. Crucially, Michael imparted to his son the significance of starting early and remaining consistent in his investment efforts. With the advantage of youth on his side, Zyon has the potential to accumulate a substantial fortune over the years through the power of compounding. By adhering to his father's advice and continuing his contributions, Zyon has the opportunity to secure his financial well-being and set himself on the path to long-term prosperity.

Indeed, as Michael's son embarks on his own financial journey, he understands that the key to success lies not in the magnitude of the initial investment, but in the commitment to starting early and remaining steadfast in his pursuit of financial growth.

Unlocking The Millionaire Lying Dormant Inside Key Takeaways

1. Mindset Matters: The foundation of wealth creation begins with a millionaire mindset—a positive attitude, a belief in abundance, and a willingness to take calculated risks.

2. Financial Literacy: Education is the key to financial empowerment. By learning about personal finance, investing, and entrepreneurship, individuals can make informed decisions and build a solid financial foundation.

3. Multiple Streams of Income: Diversifying income sources is essential for long-term financial stability. Whether through rental properties, dividend stocks, online businesses, or other ventures, creating multiple streams of income is key to building wealth.

4. Giving Back: Philanthropy and giving back to the community are integral parts of the wealth-building journey. By sharing our success and resources with others, we not only make a positive impact but also create a legacy that extends beyond ourselves.

5. Work-Life Balance: Achieving success is not just about financial gains but also about maintaining a healthy work-life balance. Prioritizing relationships, managing stress, and enjoying life outside of work are crucial for overall well-being.

6. Continued Learning: The journey towards financial independence is ongoing. Lifelong learning, continuous self-improvement, and staying informed about new opportunities are essential for sustained growth and success.

7. Persistence and Resilience: Challenges will inevitably arise on the path to wealth creation, but persistence and resilience are key. By staying focused on goals, adapting to setbacks, and never giving up, individuals can overcome obstacles and achieve their dreams.

As readers journey through the pages of "Unlock the Millionaire Lying Dormant Inside," they are invited on a transformative exploration of financial empowerment and personal growth. Within these chapters lies a wealth of wisdom, drawn not only from financial experts and successful entrepreneurs but also from the lived true experiences of individuals like Michael.

Through his story, we witness the power of resilience, determination, and a steadfast commitment to achieving one's goals. Each anecdote serves as a beacon of inspiration, illuminating the path towards financial success and fulfillment. Along the way, practical advice and actionable steps pave the way, empowering readers to take charge of their financial destinies.

From learning the basics of budgeting and saving to delving into the intricacies of stock market investing and real estate ventures, the book provides a comprehensive roadmap for building wealth and achieving financial independence. Moreover, it underscores the importance of giving back to the community and fostering meaningful connections along the journey. As readers absorb the insights shared within these pages, they are encouraged to seize the opportunity to embark on their own path towards financial abundance.

It is not merely a book to be read but a call to action, inviting readers to step into their potential, unlock their millionaire mindset, the Millionaire lurking within, and create a life of prosperity and purpose.

Dedications

This book is dedicated to all the remarkable individuals who have played a role in shaping Michael's journey towards financial success and personal growth. To his beloved mother, whose unwavering support and guidance have been a constant source of strength throughout his life. To his sister Valerie, whose steadfast encouragement has helped Michael navigate through the toughest of times. And to his wife Amal and their three children Zyon, Tia, and Tajj, whose love and inspiration have fueled Michael's determination to overcome obstacles and pursue his dreams. Additionally, this dedication extends to all the friends, family members, coaches, colleagues, and fellow soldiers who have contributed to Michael's journey in their own unique ways. Your support and encouragement have been invaluable, and for that, Michael is profoundly grateful.

To Mr. Terry Newby, Michael owes an immeasurable debt of gratitude. Without your steadfast friendship and unwavering support, Michael's path could have taken a very different, and perhaps less fortunate, turn. Your guidance, encouragement, and continued presence in Michael's life have been instrumental in shaping his journey towards success and fulfillment. Today and always, Terry, you are more than just a friend — you are a true big brother, and Michael is deeply thankful for your enduring presence in his life.

Closing Statements-Unlock The Millionaire Lying Dormant Inside

Michael is continuing his journey abroad with his wife Amal, daughter Tia, and newborn son Tajj traveling the world. As they navigate life in a new country, Michael has started a new IT services business to add to his financial goals as an entrepreneur and is looking to invest in many other international housing markets. Michael's oldest son Zyon, now 20 years old, is pursuing his dreams as a college student and working in the United States and enjoying life.

In the span of your 24-hour day, a mere single minute holds the power to alter your trajectory. Each of us encounters pivotal moments, opportunities for reflection and change, yet often these pass unnoticed or unexplored due to fear or reluctance. It's not a reflection of your capabilities, but perhaps an indication that you haven't yet ventured beyond your comfort zone. Take a moment to peer beyond the confines of familiarity, and you'll discover a world brimming with possibilities. It's never too late to make a change.

Our daily routines often lull us into a sense of complacency, blinding us to the potential for transformative change. Yet, by simply asking that one crucial question, we can unlock doors to paths we never dared to imagine. Let this serve as a gentle reminder to challenge the status quo, to embrace the unknown, and to seize the opportunities that await.

Take these words as a guiding light in your financial journey. Remember, every day presents a fresh opportunity for ordinary individuals to embark on extraordinary paths. It only takes a single step, a moment of courage, to set the wheels of change in motion and by the way, Michael and Terry have maintained a strong brotherhood, often reminiscing about their shared journey whenever they reunite. So, dare to dream, dare to ask, and dare to pursue the life you envision. The journey begins with you...

Good luck with your journey to Unlocking The Millionaire Lying Dormant Inside of you and excelling to financial freedom!

Made in the USA
Las Vegas, NV
30 May 2024

90527848R00105